Joe Kimble, Gregg Weiner and Kameshia Duncan in the City Theatre production of *Free*.

CHOOSING SIDES

SHORT PLAYS AND MONOLOGUES, COMEDIES AND DRAMAS

BY CRAIG POSPISIL

★

★

DRAMATISTS
PLAY SERVICE
INC.

2

For Caitlin Shetterly

ACKNOWLEDGMENTS

Six of these works were specifically written at the request of Caitlin Shetterly, my friend and the artistic director of the Winter Harbor Theatre Company in Portland, Maine. So it goes without saying that I thank her for forcing me ... I mean, asking me to write them. I also thank her for her patience when I went past the deadline on every one of them. And for pretty much insisting that I get back on the stage — after years away — to perform *On the Wings of a Butterfly* and then *What Price?* Caitlin is a true believer in democracy and art, and a true practitioner of both as well.

I want to thank a number of people who helped or encouraged me in the creation of some of the other plays in this collection: Larry Feeney and theAtrainplays, the 24 Hour Plays, Tony Pennino, Patricia Watt, Alex Roe and the Metropolitan Playhouse, Bruce Miller and Washington Square Arts, Jane Petrov, who acted in, produced or directed several of these, and Stephen Sultan, for his continuing support of my work.

CHOOSING SIDES

CONTENTS

ON THE WINGS
OF A BUTTERFLY

ON THE WINGS OF A BUTTERFLY was commissioned by the Winter Harbor Theater Company (Caitlin Shetterly, Artistic Director), in Portland, Maine, and performed as part of *Letters to Katrina* in December 2005. It was directed by Jane Petrov with Caitlin Shetterly, and was performed by Craig Pospisil.

The play was subsequently produced by Patricia Watt as part of *Beyond the Pale: A One-Act Festival* at the Neighborhood Playhouse in New York in May 2007. It was directed by Ari Kreith, and performed by Harris Yulin.

CHARACTERS

PLAYWRIGHT — man or woman, any age.

PLACE

An empty stage.

TIME

A few months after Hurricane Katrina hit New Orleans.

ON THE WINGS
OF A BUTTERFLY

A man, Playwright, enters. He wears a sport coat and carries a spiral bound notebook, which he places on a table or set piece. He looks out at the audience, waiting a moment before speaking.

PLAYWRIGHT.   Hello. Thank you for coming. It's good to see you here. This would be pretty lonely for me if you weren't. But here you are. Gathered in a theater, waiting for something to happen. Full of expectation.

I expect I'll disappoint you. I apologize in advance.

Convention says I stand here. In the light. You sit out there. In the dark. I speak. You listen. I tell a joke. You laugh. *(Pause, waiting for laughter.)* Thank you.

[*(Or, if they don't laugh.)* Or not.]

So, here we are. You and I. And now what? I've been asked to talk about politics and a certain hurricane that flooded New Orleans. I'm supposed to entertain you, I know. Make you feel or think. Stimulate your imagination with a lively discourse. That's what theater is about, yes?

But I'm a bit adrift these days. Actually, I'm fairly depressed, if I can be honest, so this may be a bit scattered. I thought I should warn you. If any of you would like, you can take a break for a few minutes. Go out and get a soda, a candy bar. Nice stiff drink? *(He surveys the audience. Then, almost disappointed that no one is leaving.)* You're too kind. All right, I'll begin. There's a saying about … well, it's not really a saying it's more of a … Oh, what's the word? It's not a parable. I know it's not a fable. What is it when you say something like "The journey of a thousand miles begins with a single step"?

No one? Well, it'll come to me. Or not. Starting again, the

saying goes "A butterfly in China beats its wings, and a hurricane forms in the Atlantic Ocean."

You understand? It means that small events can lead to larger ones. A cascade of moments, each triggering the next until … Seems improbable. That a stray action, say telling a lie, could lead to thousands of deaths. I mean, a butterfly couldn't cause a hurricane. Could it?

All right. Imagine a butterfly. Colorful, yellows and oranges. Put him on a flower — you pick the color — a flower on a steep hillside near Shanghai. Don't let him take off. Not yet. Make him stay there. Just flexing his wings. We'll come back to him.

Now, picture a playwright. Not Shakespeare. A living playwright. *(He looks around at the audience.)* None of you can picture a single living American playwright?

All right, forget the playwright. This may be better without one anyway. Picture yourself, then, sitting in a metal tube thirty-nine thousand, three hundred and sixty-one feet somewhere over Texas. You're on a red eye from Los Angeles to New York, returning from a trip for a long weekend. You're anxious. Not because of the turbulence, or the thunderstorm you're flying through. Or even because you're over Texas. No, that tightness in your chest is there because you've been commissioned to write something about Hurricane Katrina for a theatrical event. And it's due tomorrow morning. *(Indicating the notebook.)* But you have nothing.

Why you agreed to write something in the first place isn't important. It was a moment of weakness. You did it, it's done, and now you have to live with the consequences. Life's like that, isn't it? You've had two months to write a few paltry pages, and now the deadline — savor the word *dead*line — the deadline is imminent and you don't know what to write.

You sit there and wrack your brain for an original thought. Go ahead. I'll wait.

No? Nothing? Is it getting hard to breathe? Then it comes. An idea. You remember hearing how some of the elderly were stranded in nursing homes in New Orleans as the waters rose and the staff ran for higher ground. You get a mental picture of an old man lying asleep in a bed. See him waking up and finding himself alone, forgotten. Hear him call for help. But no one answers. The man wonders aloud, maybe reminisces about his life, calls out again for help. But no one comes, and all the while the waters rise. Now, the water is two actors kneeling on the ground downstage of him, holding opposite ends of a sheet. While the man talks, they slowly raise the sheet, until it finally covers his head ... and the man drowns.

That's a very theatrical image. You pick up your pen and start to write ... but then you stop. If he's lying there alone who is he talking to? And more to the point, who is this man? You don't know anything about him or his life. All you've got is a picture in your head.

Picture yourself putting the pen down, as the plane hits more turbulence, and the captain asks us to return to our seats and fasten our seat belts. You grit your teeth as if that will keep your inner ear from bouncing along with the rest of the plane, and you try to focus. New Orleans. What do you think of when you think of New Orleans? Besides Mardi Gras. Or "Girls Gone Wild."

All right. Imagine an empty stage. Tennessee Williams comes out and winks at the audience. He wears a light weight, light colored suit, cigarette in a cigarette holder in one hand. He smiles mischievously and in a lazy drawl says, "Blow out your candles, Mr. President."

No. Tennessee Williams? No, that's too cliché, and you don't want to just make a joke. I mean, people died.

All right. A woman is alone on a stage. She's stranded somewhere in New Orleans, surrounded by water. Waiting for rescue. She survived the hurricane, watched the levees break, struggled through the muck to find food and clean water. She got separated from her family. She wonders if they're alive or dead. She wonders if that stench is coming from the dirty water or her. And she waits for someone to find her. And waits. And finally she sees it. Two men in a boat. She jumps to her feet and runs forward as they approach, but they walk right past her, look down at the ground where she was sitting, and one says, "Here's another body."

You take out your pen and write a page or two ... until you hit the same problem you had with the elderly man. You don't know this person.

By now it's three in the morning, and you're exhausted. Turn off that little light overhead and put your seat back. One inch. Two inches. That's all you get. Sorry. Close your eyes, drift off a little ... then you sense a flash of light. You look around, but nothing. Then it happens again. Lightning in the tops of the clouds you're flying over. See yourself, nose pressed against the window, waiting for the next flash, and the next.

The clouds light up from within. Patterns of white arc through them, showing mountain ranges, valleys, rolling landscapes far above the ground. It's beautiful, like something from *Fantasia.*

Tomorrow when you turn on the television, you'll learn the tornadoes spawned by this storm killed twenty-two people. But now, here above the clouds, you can't tear your eyes away. And you wonder, what did Katrina look like from this angle? Was she beautiful too?

A flight attendant comes by with snacks. It's less than an hour 'til you land. This thing is too big to wrap your mind around. Write what you know. That's what they say. Write what you know. But what do you know of devastation and loss like that?

Well ... picture the face of the person you love the most in the world. *(Slight pause.)* No, the other one. The one who broke your heart when she said, "It's over. I'm leaving." Or words to that effect. Have you got that? The hollow feeling when everything shifts, and your world changes forever, and there's not a thing you can do to retrieve it?

Good. You look down and see that you're writing. Words spill across the page. *(Picking up the notebook.)* "We want cars to drive everywhere. Each of us in our own car. We want to be warm in the winter, and cool in the summer. We want to live in former swamps below sea level. We want to fly to Los Angeles for a long weekend. But desire is hot. So when we get what we want the world is a warmer place. And we get a hurricane season that produces more storms than letters in the alphabet. And we have to turn back to the ancient Greeks for more names. We get more category five storms in a single season than ever before, including Wilma, the most powerful hurricane ever recorded in the Atlantic, and one counter-clockwise swirling mass of air and moisture called Katrina. We're all connected; the people stranded in the Superdome and the President, tsunami victims in the Indian Ocean and victims of a suicide bomber in Baghdad. People starving in the Sudan, and people on line at the local McDonalds. Me. You.

So is Katrina to blame for the ruined lives? Is the president? The man who ran FEMA? The butterfly? Or, like that failed relationship, did you maybe have a hand in it?"

Well, it's a theory.

Let's go back to China and our butterfly, is he still … An adage! It's an adage. Well, I feel better. So, our butterfly. Is he still sitting on that flower? Let him take off, fly to the next one. Has he gone? How many wing beats did it take? Did he start any hurricanes?

Well, I wouldn't worry about butterflies. They'll probably all be gone soon. And then who will we blame? *(The Playwright exits with his notebook, as the lights fade to black.)*

End of Play

FREE

FREE was originally produced by AtrainProductions (Lawrence Feeney, Executive Producer) as part of *theAtrainplays, Vol. 14* at the Neighborhood Playhouse, in New York City, in March 2004. It was directed by Daniel Ruth. It was later produced as part of *theAtrain(re)plays: The Best of theAtrainplays* at the Peter J. Sharp Theatre at Playwrights Horizons, in New York City, in March 2005. It was directed by Mark Lonergan. The cast for both productions was as follows:

STEVE .... Scott Wood
LILI .... Lisa Barnes
DEREK .... David Mitchell

FREE was subsequently produced by City Theatre, in Miami, Florida, as part of their *Summer Shorts* series in June 1, 2006. It was directed by Kim St. Leon. The cast was as follows:

STEVE .... Joe Kimble
LILI .... Kameshia Duncan
DEREK .... Gregg Weiner

CHARACTERS

STEVE — a man having a panic attack.
LILI — a nervous woman.
DEREK — her boyfriend.

PLACE

A New York City subway car.

TIME

The present.

FREE

A New York subway car, the A train. Steve enters from the platform. He's dressed in a jacket and tie and carries a briefcase. He is jittery and extremely nervous. He sits. He stands. He sits. He stands, paces. He claws at his tie, loosening it. Then pulling it off. He sits. He stands, wipes sweat off his brow. He takes off his jacket. He's been sweating and his shirt is damp. He loosens a couple buttons and tries to air himself out.

He sits, tries to relax. Can't find a comfortable position. His throat closes up on him and he chokes, having an anxiety attack. He jumps to his feet, pulling off his shirt and tossing it on the bench.

He stops and looks at the growing pile of clothes on the bench. He thinks. He looks in the next car. He looks at his clothes. He thinks.

Steve quickly sits and pulls off his shoes and socks. He holds his feet up in the air then lowers them to the floor. He laughs. He gets up and takes a few tentative steps around the car. He's thrilled. He checks the other car. Still no one.

He looks down at his pants. He looks in the next car. He looks down at his pants, and then quickly — before he can change his mind — he takes them off and tosses them on the bench.

He looks around and can't believe it. He laughs and struts around the car, triumphantly. He smiles and walks back to the bench, ready to put his clothes back on.. He stops, looks down at his underwear.

Steve looks very carefully into the next car. He looks down at his underwear. He pulls at the elastic and looks inside. He checks the other car again, takes a deep breath and in one very quick motion pulls his underwear down to his ankles and stands up, raising his arms in triumph over his head.

STEVE. Yes!!! *(Then he quickly bends down pulls up his underwear and collapses back on the bench. Suddenly he lurches as the train begins to slow into the next station. He desperately tries to gather up his clothes. He maybe gets one arm in a shirt, but mainly sits with his briefcase and clothes covering his lap as Lili and Derek enter.)*

LILI. I don't want to talk about it.

DEREK. Lil, you need to speak up for yourself. You're the best person in that office. You deserve that promotion. *(Steve tries to remain motionless or maybe he tries to very slowly pull on some piece of clothing while Lili and Derek talk, standing at one of the poles.)*

LILI. Well, that may be, but I didn't get it, so what can I do?

DEREK. Quit.

LILI. I can't do that!

DEREK. Honey, you have to. You've got to take a stand and tell them, "I won't be pushed around." If you don't they'll keep taking you for granted. But if you threaten to quit, it'll scare them.

LILI. It'll scare me. You know how much my rent is. If I quit, I wouldn't last … *(She and Derek stop as they suddenly register the fact that there's an almost naked man on the train with them. They turn slowly and look at him.)*

STEVE. Hi.

LILI. Oh my God!

DEREK. What the hell.

STEVE. I suppose you're wondering why I'm not wearing … much.

LILI. Stay away from us.

STEVE. No, don't worry. I'm not going to do anything.

DEREK. You damn well better not.

STEVE. I won't.

LILI. I'll scream.

STEVE. No, no, please don't! I won't do anything. I swear.

DEREK. *(Pause.)* Why aren't you wearing any clothes?

STEVE. Well, actually, I'm still wearing —

DEREK. Just answer the question.

22

STEVE. Well, that's … it's kind of an odd … I mean, it's funny, not … you'll laugh really, because … I'm not entirely sure.

LILI. You don't know?

DEREK. Your clothes just fell off your body?

STEVE. No, no, you see, I didn't plan to, but … I was alone.

LILI. So?

STEVE. Well, it's one of those things that just happens sometimes. I mean … don't you ever, you know, take all your clothes off when you're alone?

DEREK. Are you a pervert?

STEVE. No, I'm just saying.

LILI. Well, everyone takes their clothes off when they're alone. At home. With the doors locked. And all the lights off.

DEREK. But not on the subway!

STEVE. Okay, yes, but all I'm trying to say is —

DEREK. You *are* a pervert.

LILI. Derek, let him finish.

DEREK. Excuse me?

LILI. I … I just mean, he's trying to explain and all, but … never mind.

STEVE. Look, it all … it just kind of happened. It's been a long day, and I've been … I was overheating, and I couldn't breathe, and —

DEREK. Oh, come on! Everyone has bad days, but … are you going to get dressed or what?!

STEVE. Oh! Of course.

DEREK. Then don't let me stop you! *(Steve starts to get dressed, but then stops.)*

STEVE. Or maybe I won't.

DEREK. What?

STEVE. I said, or maybe I won't.

LILI. I can still scream

STEVE. Fine, go ahead.

DEREK. Okay, what's going on? Is this some kind of joke? Some reality TV thing? Hmm? Why'd you take off your clothes?

STEVE. I wanted to feel free.

DEREK. Free?

STEVE. Yeah.

DEREK. That's fucked up.

STEVE. No, it's not. It's liberating. And right now … I feel like I could do anything.

DEREK. I think it's time you felt like putting your clothes on. *(Steve laughs.)*
LILI. What's so funny?
STEVE. It's not what you think it is. It's not about sex. Look, if you're scared, go into the other car.
DEREK. I'm not scared of you!
STEVE. I'm not going to do anything or try anything or expose myself.
LILI. You're exposed right now.
STEVE. No, I'm not. In fact ... I may not even legally be naked right now.
DEREK. Are you kidding me?
STEVE. I'm wearing as much as that guy who plays guitar in Times Square.
LILI. You mean, the *Naked* Cowboy?
STEVE. Oh, that's just his name. If it was illegal, they'd arrest him, right? But they don't. And all he wears is his underwear.
DEREK. And cowboy boots.
STEVE. You want me to put my shoes on?
LILI. How can you walk around on this floor in your bare feet?
STEVE. It's very soft actually.
LILI. But it's filthy.
STEVE. So, I'll wash my feet when I get home.
DEREK. You know what, I've had it. Stay naked. I'm getting a cop.
LILI. Why?
DEREK. Why?! He's a pervert!
LILI. He seems harmless. I mean, he hasn't done anything.
DEREK. Oh, come on! I mean ... he's naked and he's ... he's ... oh, this is nuts. He's nuts.
LILI. I just think you're overreacting a bit, honey.
DEREK. This from the woman who never reacts.
LILI. What?
DEREK. You never react to anything. You never fight back. You don't get what you should, but all you say is, "Oh, well. I guess there's nothing I can do."
LILI. Derek, I ... I ...
DEREK. You what? Hmm? What? See? I'm getting a cop. *(He turns to leave.)* Are you coming?
LILI. No.

DEREK. Lil … look, I'm sorry I snapped, but …

LILI. Just go. I'll be all right. I've got my pepper spray.

DEREK. Fine. *(To Steve.)* I'll be right back. *(Derek exits. Lili sits. Steve starts to get dressed.)*

STEVE. I'm sorry. I didn't mean to start a fight.

LILI. No. I … Why did you take your clothes off?

STEVE. *(Pause.)* I was afraid.

LILI. Of what?

STEVE. I … I was having this massive panic attack. All day I've been really light headed and … see, I've been dating this woman for a long time and … and it's great, you know? It's terrific. So a couple months ago I started thinking, "We should get married. Her birthday's coming up. I'll ask her then." *(Slight pause.)* Well, today's her birthday, I've got a ring for her here in my briefcase … and I'm scared out of my mind. Every time I start to think about what I'm actually going to say … my throat closes up and I start to choke and I break into a cold sweat and … I was just trying to get some air, and I took off my shirt and tie … and I saw them lying there and I thought, if I could get naked on the A train, if I could do that … there'd be nothing I couldn't do.

LILI. And? Do you think it worked?

STEVE. I don't know. Maybe. I feel pretty amazing. *(Pause.)* You want to try it?

LILI. Oh, no! I couldn't.

STEVE. I wouldn't have thought I could.

LILI. No.

STEVE. I'll watch the door.

LILI. What?

STEVE. I'll watch the door to see if anyone's coming. We're in the last car. That's the only way they could come.

LILI. I couldn't get undressed in front of you.

STEVE. I'll keep my back turned. Really.

LILI. No, it wouldn't matter. I wouldn't be alone. You said you had to be alone.

STEVE. No, I said I was alone. It doesn't have to be that way. I don't think there are any rules about this. So? *(Lili thinks. She nods at him. He goes to the door and watches, his back to her. She watches him for a moment and then steps into the middle of the car and steels herself.)*

LILI. No one's coming?

STEVE. No. You're good. *(She takes off her overcoat and lets it fall to the ground.)* Still no one coming.

LILI. I didn't ask.

STEVE. I'm just saying.

LILI. Well, don't say anything unless I ask.

STEVE. Okay. *(She peels off the rest of her clothes and stands there in her bra and panties for a moment, reveling in the experience for a few moments. Then she smiles and starts to dress again.)*

LILI. Okay.

STEVE. *(Turning back to her.)* That's it?

LILI. It was enough.

STEVE. How do you feel?

LILI. Fine.

STEVE. Just fine?

LILI. Fine is ... pretty good.

STEVE. Good.

LILI. How do you feel?

STEVE. Me? Like I can breathe. *(Slight pause.)* And here's her stop.

LILI. Good luck.

STEVE. You too. *(Steve steps off the train and quickly disappears. After a moment Derek reenters from the other car.)*

DEREK. There is never a cop on these trains! But I told the ... Where'd he go?

LILI. He got off.

DEREK. Damn it! That guy should not be ... *(Seeing her shoes on the floor.)* What's going on here?

LILI. Just a little experiment.

DEREK. What?! Did he...? Did you...? Are you telling me...?

LILI. Uh-huh.

DEREK. Lili! Are you crazy? *(She gets up and picks up her shoes.)*

LILI. Oh, I hope so.

DEREK. What? This is ... this ... we're going to have to talk about this.

LILI. No. *(She feels the floor of the train with one bare foot. Smiles.)* You know ... it is soft. *(She walks off the train barefoot, followed by Derek.)*

DEREK. Lili? Wait a minute ... Lili?

End of Play

WHAT PRICE?

WHAT PRICE? was commissioned by the Winter Harbor Theater Company (Caitlin Shetterly, Artistic Director), in Portland, Maine, and performed as part of its production *Letters to Baghdad* in June 2006. It was directed by Caitlin Shetterly. The cast was as follows:

BETH .... Farah Bala
MAN .... Craig Pospisil

WHAT PRICE? was first produced in New York by 3Graces Theater Company as part of *Spring Shorts 2*, opening on April 6, 2008. It was directed by Margot Avery. The cast was as follows:

BETH .... Suzanne Barbetta
MAN .... Brian McFadden

CHARACTERS

BETH — a woman in her thirties or forties.
MAN — a government official.

PLACE

A nondescript interrogation room.

TIME

The future?

WHAT PRICE?

A woman, Beth, sits alone in a stark room that looks very much like a police interrogation room. Another chair and metal table are also here.

Beth waits. She looks at her watch. Waits. She looks at the door, then nervously around the room. She waits.

A man enters, carrying a file folder and a recording device. He pays no attention to the woman, who sits up quickly. He crosses to the table and sits in the other chair. He opens the folder and reviews the first couple of pages, still not acknowledging the woman.

The woman looks on anxiously. She opens her mouth to speak and the man suddenly lifts a single finger in the air, signaling her to stay quiet. He continues to read. Then man takes out a pen and turns on the recorder. He continues to read the file.

MAN. *(Abruptly.)* Name?
BETH. My…? Don't you have that?
MAN. What is your name?
BETH. It's Freeman. Beth Freeman. *(The man writes something, and continues to review his file.)* It's just I wrote it on the top of the forms, so I thought you'd have that. You had me worried I was in the wrong room, or that —
MAN. This'll go better if you just answer the questions.
BETH. *(Pause.)* All right.
MAN. Age?
BETH. Didn't I write that … *(She trails off on his look.)* I'm *[age]*.
MAN. *(Turning off the recorder.)* Are you going to keep doing that?
BETH. No, I'm sorry.

MAN. Are you sure?

BETH. Yes.

MAN. *(He turns the recorder on and goes back to his notes.)* You're married.

BETH. Yes.

MAN. Your husband's name?

BETH. Michael Williams. *(Man stops writing, looks at her.)* I kept my name.

MAN. *(Looks at her a moment longer.)* You have children?

BETH. Yes. Danielle and Sarah.

MAN. And their last names?

BETH. *(Slight pause.)* Williams. *(Slight pause.)* What does all this have to do with —

MAN. Just answer the questions, please.

BETH. But they don't have anything to do with —

MAN. They're entirely relevant to what we need to know.

BETH. But why do you need names of my children?

MAN. Are you going to cooperate here?

BETH. No. I mean, I am. I will. Yes.

MAN. Then all you have to do is answer the questions as succinctly as possible. All right?

BETH. Yes, all right.

MAN. Have you ever been convicted of a crime?

BETH. A — ? No.

MAN. Ever been arrested?

BETH. No.

MAN. Investigated for any reason?

BETH. No. *(Man just stares at her.)* Oh. Well, we were audited a couple years ago. We made a ... subtracted wrong. But we took care of it. Paid a small penalty.

MAN. Occupation?

BETH. I do graphic design work for a firm north of Boston.

MAN. That's a long commute from Portland.

BETH. Yeah, it ... when I started it was only a couple days a week and Michael was working in Bath, so it wasn't so bad, but ... Michael got laid off recently, so I've had to go to full time.

MAN. You could move.

BETH. The girls are in a good school here, and we've got family in the area.

MAN. Mmm. Religion?

BETH. Excuse me?

MAN. What's your religious background.

BETH. Is it legal for you to ask me that? *(Man looks at her, then writes something.)* What are you writing?

MAN. Were you born an American citizen?

BETH. Yes. I was born here in Maine. In Portland.

MAN. And you've traveled outside the U.S.?

BETH. Of course.

MAN. Of course?

BETH. Yeah. Why not?

MAN. You've made trips to England, France ... Morocco.

BETH. Yeah.

MAN. And phone records indicate quite a few international calls to Morocco. Two or three a month.

BETH. How do you know about my phone calls?

MAN. Who are you calling?

BETH. You can't ask me questions like that. I want a lawyer.

MAN. You don't get one here. Who are you calling?

BETH. What, are we at war with them now?

MAN. I don't think you want to be glib with me.

BETH. I'm calling my sister, okay? She lives there. She married a Moroccan. Is it all right if I call her?

MAN. Do you frequently consort with foreign nationals?

BETH. I don't believe this.

MAN. Are you a loyal American citizen?

BETH. Going to Casablanca doesn't make me disloyal.

MAN. What about sedition?

BETH. Sedition?

MAN. The organized incitement of rebellion or civil disorder against the state.

BETH. Civil disorder? Are you ... I don't understand. What about it?

MAN. Have you ever participated in seditious acts?

BETH. Me? No.

MAN. No? *(Refers to his files.)* January, three years ago, you attend-ed a protest march in New York against the war. July of —

BETH. A march isn't ... How'd you know about that?

MAN. We know a great deal.

BETH. Wait are ... are you investigating me?

MAN. *(Turning off the recorder.)* We're not after you.

BETH. What is this?

MAN. We need a name. One name. That's all.

BETH. A name?

MAN. Someone who's threatened the fabric of the nation.

BETH. I don't know anyone like that.

MAN. Of course you do. We all do.

BETH. No, really. I don't. I'm not very political. I went to a couple marches, but …

MAN. So you've never heard anyone, say, call the war "immoral"?

BETH. No.

MAN. … call the President a "liar"?

BETH. No.

MAN. *(Reading from his notes.)* … or say the war was "a gift of new oil fields to the companies that helped buy the presidency"?

BETH. *(Starting to answer, then recognizing the phrase.)* N-No, I'm sorry. *(The Man looks at her for a moment. Then he flips through his file until he finds the information he wants.)*

MAN. Your children attend the Wainfleet School. Sarah is in pre-kindergarten. Danielle in first grade, and gets good marks in math. She was nervous about starting school and clung to your pant leg when you took her there for the first day. It is now 11:30 which means Danielle's about to start gym class. She's learning to swim. *(Slight pause.)* That's a good thing. The water can be dangerous if you don't know how.

BETH. What are you doing?

MAN. My job.

BETH. By threatening a little girl?

MAN. Mrs. Williams, you know very well I'm not threatening your daughter.

BETH. Please don't.

MAN. I just need a name.

BETH. Don't.

MAN. One name.

BETH. No.

MAN. Maybe I should call the school to check on Danielle. *(He pulls a cell phone out of his pocket.)*

BETH. No.

MAN. You don't want me to call the school?

BETH. No.

MAN. *(Starting to dial the phone.)* I think I should.

BETH. No, this isn't right! You've got no right to ask me these questions, to do this. You don't have this power.

MAN. Then you shouldn't have given it to me.

BETH. What?

MAN. I didn't ask you to come in here today. You came in of your own free will because you wanted something. You can leave at any time.

BETH. No, please! I can't! I need —

MAN. So, you want to stay?

BETH. *(Pause.)* Yes.

MAN. And you'll answer my question?

BETH. *(Quietly.)* Yes.

MAN. What was that?

BETH. I'll answer your question. *(The man turns the recorder on again.)*

MAN. Have you ever heard anyone you know make openly seditious statements?

BETH. Yes.

MAN. Who was that person?

BETH. Michael Williams.

MAN. Your husband.

BETH. Yes.

MAN. Thank you. *(Turns off the recorder.)* Now, was that so hard?

BETH. So, does this mean...?

MAN. Yes. We'll take care of everything from here.

BETH. Oh my God. Wait, are you going to — ?

MAN. *(Interrupting.)* How much do you need? *(Beth just looks at him, stunned.)* I've got people waiting. Cars lined up around the corner. How much do you need?

BETH. *(Stammering.)* I ... I need to fill the tank. We need ... I've got to get the girls from school ... and groceries, and there's work tomorrow. I have to drive to Boston *(As she speaks the man finishes his paperwork. He signs off on the form and crosses to her, holding it out.)*

MAN. Fine. You're in luck. The price has come down to fifteen dollars a gallon. You can pay at the pump. *(Blackout.)*

End of Play

NO CHILD LEFT

NO CHILD LEFT was commissioned by the Winter Harbor Theater Company (Caitlin Shetterly, Artistic Director), in Portland, Maine, and performed as part of *Letters to Ohio* in March 2005. It was directed by Caitlin Shetterly, and was performed by Denise Poirier.

The play was subsequently produced by Patricia Watt as part of *Beyond the Pale: A One-Act Festival* at the Neighborhood Playhouse in New York in May 2007. It was performed by Kristin Lowman.

CHARACTERS

MRS. O'REILLY — a school teacher.

PLACE

A classroom.

TIME

The present.

NO CHILD LEFT

*Mrs. O'Reilly, a primly dressed woman, enters with an arm-
load of books. She smiles out to the audience.*

MRS. O'REILLY. Good morning, class. I hope you all had a nice
vacation. I'm your new teacher, Mrs. O'Reilly, and I'm so happy to
be here, shaping your young minds. What? No, Miss Lincoln won't
be coming back. No, I don't know why, but I'm sure it had nothing
to do with her remarks about the President. And I'm certainly not
going to spread any of those awful rumors that she's a drug
addicted whore.

Now, there are some very exciting changes here at school, and
it's all thanks to the President, who doesn't want any of you to be
left behind. Isn't that wonderful?

The first thing you should know is there will be a lot of tests
coming up, and those of you who don't do well on those tests will
be responsible when the government cuts funding for this school.
But let's not dwell on which of you will be ruining things for everyone else. First, I want everyone to get out their old text books,
because we need to go over some of the changes, so we can be pre-
pared to answer the President's question: Is our children learning?

All right, let's start with English, which is very important,
because we all need it to be able to read and write and even talk.
Isn't that right, Jose? Habla Ingles? Oh, you do? Well, what a surprise.

Now, in the past people made English much harder than it
needed to be. This year I'll teach you that the great thing about
English is that it's so adaptablistic. Now, I bet some of you are
thinking, "Hey, 'adaptablistic' isn't a word." But you're wrong.
Because one of the new things you'll learn is that it's all right to
make up new words.

From now on, if you squish a couple words together or add
extra syllables, but people can still guesstigate what you mean, then

you've invented a new word. And you'll get extra credit for that. And it doesn't mean you're stupid, or that you're trying to duck a question from some reporter.

English is hard. Just ask little Juan up here. Hmm? Right, right, Jose, whatever. I mean, don't we know what someone means when they say, "Teach a child to read, and he or her will be able to pass a literacy test"? Of course we do.

All right, let's move on to history. Have you ever wondered how we know what really happened in the past? Is it just because somebody wrote something down? What if history books were written by angry, bitter people, like Democrats, who didn't get to turn America into a godless, socialist nightmare and decided to make up stuff? Wouldn't it be awful if we taught you things that weren't true?

You bet it would. And that's why our school has ordered new history books written by the fair and balanced people at Fox News. They'll tell you what really happened all those years ago in Vietnam and Iraq, and what's a lot of nonsense made up by sore losers.

Okay, next is math. Now you might think, "Math is math. It can't change" but you'd be as wrong as the Democrats, who think life isn't sacred and want to kill little babies not much younger than you. The new thing I'll teach you is that everything is the opposite of what it seems.

For example, I'm sure you've all heard of the economy. Can anyone tell me what it is? Put your hand down, Jose. When people talk about the economy what they mean is, "How much money do your mommy and daddy have?" Now a few years ago, our government had what's called a surplus. That's from Latin. "Sur" meaning "above" or "beyond" and "plus" meaning "plus." Back then America had double plus more money than it needed. That's a very good thing for a person or for a business, but it's very bad for a country. When a country has extra money it wastes it protecting butterfly habitats, or teaching sex education, when all you need to know is that if you have sex before marriage you'll die and go to hell.

Thankfully, the President decided to make the government steal less from your mommy and daddy, and spend more on important things, like subsidizing oil companies, who need our help so badly. And now America has a deficit, which means we don't have enough money to pay for things and have to borrow money to be able to bail out companies on Wall Street. And that's good, because it means money is out in the economy as God intended. Which is why our money says, "In God we trust." So, in short, positive is negative and negative is positive, okay?

Let's move on. Science … well, the less said about that the better. This book is filled with more unfacts than a filibustering Democrat. Just look at the table of contents: "Darwin and Evolution," "The Big Bang," "Global Warming." It just makes me want to vomit. I'd ask you to rip out those pages, but there'd be nothing left. So just throw the whole book away and pick up your new text book. Did you all find a copy on your desks? It's the book labeled "the Holy Bible"? Yes? Good.

What's that, Rachel? Religion? Well, yes, it is religion. It's also the bedrock this nation was founded on. What? The Constitution? I don't think I like your tone, young lady. In fact, I think you'd better march right down to the principal's office so he can call your parents and tell them you've been suspended. That's right, get going. Move it!

Anyone else? I didn't think so.

Sorry about that, boys and girls. It's always upsetting to find there are people in this country who just don't love America. Maybe someday we'll be able to deport them.

Now, before we get started, please stand and join me in reciting the Pledge of Allegiance. The new words are posted on the wall. Right next to the Ten Commandments. *(She places her right hand over her heart.)* I pledge allegiance to the God of the United States of America, and to the Right public which stands Him up, one nation, with one god, united, not divided, with liberty and justice for thine is the kingdom, and the power and the glory, for ever and ever. Amen. *(She holds as the lights fade to black.)*

End of Play

GUERILLA GORILLA

GUERILLA GORILLA was commissioned by Gorilla Rep, and was produced as part of *Washington Square Dreams* in New York on October 30, 2001. It was directed by Anthony Pennino. The cast was as follows:

TINA .... Katherine Gooch
ALANA .... Rachel Jackson
SANDY .... Dale Ho
MUTTON .... Sean Elias-Reyes

CHARACTERS

TINA — a police officer.

ALANA — a young woman, loves the theater.

SANDY — a young man, in love with Alana.

MUTTON — looks like a drug dealer.

PLACE

Washington Square Park, New York.

TIME

The not too distant future.

GUERILLA GORILLA

Washington Square Park in the near future. It is night. Shadows flicker across a park bench and the surrounding bushes as a brilliant moon shines through the leaves of the trees overhead. Tina, a police officer, patrols through the area. She stops, as if sensing something, but after looking over the area she continues on. A young man and woman, Sandy and Alana, sneak out from behind some bushes. They look about furtively.

SANDY. Come on. Please. Let's get out of here.

ALANA. No, Sandy. Look, you can go home, but I want to see Danny in this play.

SANDY. The park is dangerous. I'm not leaving you alone here.

ALANA. Well, I didn't ask you to come, or to follow me like some stray dog.

SANDY. This is illegal. We're gonna get caught.

ALANA. No, we're not. The cops don't care. It's a stupid law and they know it. Like jaywalking. No one pays attention.

SANDY. Alana, they bust people all the time for theater-going. I read on the internet that forty people got arrested in one night last summer for going to a play.

ALANA. Yeah, I saw that too. But those people were asking for it. That was stupid, putting on a play in the middle of Central Park. Of course you're gonna get caught. But this group, Gorilla Rep, they move around. They're harder to spot.

SANDY. Hello?! We just missed getting spotted by that cop!

ALANA. But she *did* miss us.

SANDY. This is insane.

ALANA. It's not like it hurts anyone.

SANDY. That's not the point.

ALANA. Of course it's the point. It's stupid to outlaw something that doesn't hurt anyone. Something, in fact, that lots of people enjoy.

SANDY. No, the point is that live theater is illegal now. It doesn't matter if the law is good or bad. You can be arrested for performing or just watching a play. And they're really serious about prosecuting people. *(Slight pause.)* And it's not like anyone needs theater anymore. Between cable and the internet, people can get all the entertainment they need at home. Safe. Theaters are just places where people might get hurt.

ALANA. How?

SANDY. Lots of ways. Like … fires, or … riots.

ALANA. Riots?!

SANDY. It's happened. And any time people are in the same place there's the chance of the spread of disease, or —

ALANA. Oh, please, you can't believe that stuff! The government just made up all that nonsense because the theater scares them. It expresses the truths about this corrupt society, and it's something they couldn't control. They tried to kill it by abolishing the NEA, but it kept going. So they passed this absurd law.

SANDY. Alana, are you listening to yourself? You sound like one of those radicals from the Sixties, or … Oh, I am so stupid. Danny. He fed you all that, right?

ALANA. Hey, Danny's right. Theater's dangerous to the status quo. It's political and alive. You never know what might happen.

SANDY. I know what's going to happen. We're gonna spend the night in jail.

ALANA. So go home where it's nice and safe and no one's rioting. I'm seeing Danny's play.

SANDY. He's gay, you know.

ALANA. *(Slight pause.)* What does that have to do with anything?

SANDY. It means, he's gay. He likes men. You are a woman. He's not interested in you like that.

ALANA. I just want to see a play.

SANDY. Please! You think I don't know you're in love with him?

ALANA. I am not.

SANDY. It's so obvious! You hang on his every word, and get all —

ALANA. Nobody asked for your opinion! You don't know what you're talking about.

SANDY. I know you're making an ass of yourself!

ALANA. Hey, you wanna keep it down? If you keep shouting like that and we *will* get arrested.

SANDY. I wasn't shouting.

ALANA. Oh, would you just go! You don't want to be here, and I don't want you around if you're gonna be so judgmental.

SANDY. Alana — *(Mutton, a scruffy looking man, slides into the scene.)*

MUTTON. Tix. Tix. I got tix. Who wants 'em?

SANDY. What?

MUTTON. Tix, man. I got tix.

SANDY. *(To Alana.)* Ticks?

ALANA. Tickets, Sandy.

MUTTON. You guys wanna see a show?

ALANA. Yeah, what've you got?

MUTTON. Well, lemme see. I got some quality *Godot* goin' down in Tribeca, a *Streetcar* over on the Bowery, or *Midsummer Night's Dream* right here in the park.

ALANA. How much for *Midsummer*?

MUTTON. Whoo-whee. Girl likes the hot stuff.

ALANA. Yeah, yeah. How much?

MUTTON. Well, it's gonna cost you. I mean, this is high profile stuff here. And Shakespeare to boot.

ALANA. Hey, quality's worth the price.

MUTTON. Right you are. Okay. *Midsummer's* gonna set you back thirty a tick.

ALANA. Thirty?

SANDY. You've gotta be kidding!

MUTTON. Hey, if the price is too steep, I've got other shows. I got a lead on some cheap Neil Simon in Queens.

ALANA. No, no, I want *Midsummer*.

MUTTON. You sure?

ALANA. Yeah. Two tix.

MUTTON. Okay. You hang out here. I'll go pick a couple good ones outta my stash. *(Mutton quickly slinks away.)*

ALANA. I need twenty bucks.

SANDY. What?

ALANA. I didn't think the tix would be so much. I need twenty bucks. *(Slight pause.)* Come on, Sandy. It'll be fun. Live a little. *(Sandy digs in his pockets and gives Alana some money.)*

SANDY. Okay.

ALANA. Thanks. You'll like it. Really. It's like nothing you've ever seen on TV.

SANDY. I'm just nervous. Where'd he go? Doesn't he have the

tickets on him?

ALANA. Are you kidding? They don't carry the tix around. What if he's holding and he gets busted? He'd lose the whole stash. They hide them somewhere, and they only get them out when they're making a sale. Plus if we were Theater Narcs and we bought a couple of tix from him, that's just a misdemeanor. He'd be back on the street in a couple of hours. But if he was holding ten, twelve tix … that's a felony.

SANDY. Something just doesn't feel right.

ALANA. Do you want your money back? I can go alone.

SANDY. Why won't you give me a chance?

ALANA. Sandy … I really value you as a friend, but I just can't see us as a couple. We've got really different outlooks. I mean, like, right here. I love things like this, but you'd rather be on your couch watching a movie. And that's fine, but it's not for me. *(Mutton re-enters.)*

MUTTON. Okay, I got your tix. You got the money?

ALANA. Right here. *(Alana hands the money over to Mutton, who pockets it, smiles and pulls out a badge, which he holds up.)*

MUTTON. And you are busted.

ALANA. What?

SANDY. I knew it!! *(Tina, the cop, enters, gun drawn.)*

TINA. Good catch, Mutton.

ALANA. Damn it!

MUTTON. You are under arrest for breaking Article Five, section four of the state penal code, attempting to witness a live theatrical event.

SANDY. Officer, please. This is a first offense. We'll never do it again, I swear. Couldn't you let us off with a warning?

ALANA. Speak for yourself! I'll do it again! The theater is a valid form of artistic expression. It doesn't hurt anyone*! (Mutton turns on Alana. His anger rises steadily as he talks, and he closes in on her.)*

MUTTON. The theater doesn't hurt anyone? How fucking naïve are you?! Families all across America are torn apart by the specter of the theater every day. Have you ever seen first hand what the theater can do to a family? I've looked into the eyes of parents who were crushed when their children came home one day and said, "I want to be an actor." I've seen what happens to those actors when they found they couldn't make a living and turned to prostitution or waiting tables. Eventually they're forced to give up and become teachers. They fall into a depression and need years of psychotherapy.

You think about the thousands of people whose lives have been destroyed by the dream of "the Theater"! And then you try to tell me that it's a victimless crime!! *(Tina takes hold of Mutton's arm and pulls him back.)*

TINA. Mutton, hey, take it easy. She's young.

MUTTON. Yeah, I know, I know. It just makes me crazy. I can't stop thinking what fools these people are.

TINA. Well, they'll have some time to think about it in jail. You keep 'em here. I'll bring the van around. *(Tina exits. Mutton takes out a pair of handcuffs and approaches Alana.)*

MUTTON. Turn around. Hands behind your back. *(Sandy suddenly pulls a small canister of pepper spray from his pocket and sprays Mutton in the face. Mutton immediately recoils, screaming in pain and holding his hands over his eyes.)*

MUTTON. Aahh!!!

SANDY. Run!! *(Sandy grabs Alana and pulls her back into the bushes. Tina races back in, gun drawn. Mutton squints through his tears, looking in all directions.)*

TINA. Mutton! You okay?

MUTTON. I will be. When I kick that guy's ass. Did you see which way they went?

TINA. That way, I think. *(Tina and Mutton run off. After a moment, Sandy and Alana emerge from the bushes.)*

ALANA. Wow. That was ... you were incredible.

SANDY. I couldn't let him arrest you.

ALANA. What were you doing with that pepper spray?

SANDY. I told you this park was dangerous. I never go outside without it.

ALANA. I just never thought you'd ... that you would do something so dangerous. You're always so practical, reasonable.

SANDY. Well ... reason and love don't always mix.

ALANA. Yeah. *(Slight pause.)* I guess we should get out of here. Wanna go home and watch some TV?

SANDY. Hell, no. I've never felt so alive. Let's find that play! *(They run off, holding hands. Blackout.)*

End of Play

TRAIN OF THOUGHT

TRAIN OF THOUGHT was originally produced in the *Cold Reading Series* by Sarah Bisman and Philip Naudé and the 24 Hour Company at the Brooklyn Academy of Music on January 23, 2005. The cast was as follows:

WADE .... Laurence Winslow
NINA .... Nancy Wu
FRANK .... Lawrence Feeney
MARCY .... Megan Leigh

TRAIN OF THOUGHT was subsequently staged by the Playwrights Actors Contemporary Theatre (Jane Petrov, Artistic Director) as part of *Fully PACT* in New York in November 2005. It was directed by Chris Maring. The cast was as follows:

WADE .... Scott Katzman
NINA .... Nancy Wu
FRANK .... Michael Rhodes
MARCY .... Missy Hall

CHARACTERS

WADE — a man obsessed with a woman on the train.

NINA — a woman unnerved by Wade's stare.

FRANK — Nina's boyfriend.

MARCY — Wade's girlfriend.

PLACE

A New York City subway car.

TIME

The present.

TRAIN OF THOUGHT

A New York subway car. Two couples, Wade & Marcy and Nina & Frank, sit at opposite ends of the car. Wade looks down the car and sees Nina. He stares at her, transfixed. Nina sees this. She looks back at him for a moment and then away. Marcy glances at Wade and then reads the ads on the walls of the train. Frank reads a newspaper. Unless otherwise specified, they speak out to the audience.

WADE. I see her at the other end of the train. She's with someone, and so am I, but … well, our eyes meet, and something happens. There's an immediate connection between us. It jumps out, arcs across the car like lightning, and I feel this leap in my chest. *(Slight pause.)* I know how this sounds. I mean, it's ridiculous. Love at first sight? "Our eyes met across a crowded train and in that instant I knew … " I mean, come on. It just doesn't happen. *(Slight pause.)* But there it is. And from the way she looks back at me … I know she feels it too.

NINA. This guy at the other end of the train keeps looking at me … and it's creeping me out. I mean, I'm sitting here with my boyfriend, and this guy keeps staring at me. *(Slight pause.)* And he's with some woman! And she looks nice, and I start to feel sorry for her, 'cause she looks happy and all, but her boyfriend is a total freak. And I want to jump up and shout, "Don't you see what your boyfriend's doing?" *(Slight pause.)* But I don't, of course. And she doesn't seem to notice. So, I snuggle closer to Frank and try to think of something else. I think about how lucky I am to be with someone who loves me and wouldn't do creepy things like stare at other women. And how much I like to be held by him. *(Slight pause.)* But I know this guy is there, and I can feel his eyes are still on me. I glance his way to be sure … and he is! He's still staring. And he smiles at me!!! What an asshole! *(Slight pause.)* I'm glad

Frank is here. I take hold of his hand and give it a squeeze.

FRANK. I don't want to go home with Nina tonight. And I don't want her coming to my place. I want to spend the night alone. Is that all right? I just want to go home and go to sleep. I wouldn't be sitting with her on the train now if we didn't both live downtown, but ... *(Slight pause.)* That dinner was awful. I fuckin' hate sushi. Raw fish? I mean, you've gotta be kidding me. We're not supposed to eat raw meat. That's why we invented ovens, right? The tuna's okay most of the time, I guess. That's the only one I can stand. It kinda melts in your mouth, and if you put enough soy sauce on it, it goes down okay. But, man, I thought I was going to puke from whatever that white fish was. Jesus! I mean, that just sat there in my mouth, and I'm chewing and chewing, and suddenly it pops into my head, "Dude, you've got raw fish in your mouth." I don't know how I swallowed that. No more. No more freaking sushi!

WADE. This is driving me crazy! It's like I'm in prison. And freedom is just twenty feet away. I'm so drawn to her. She's amazing looking. But what can I do? *(Slight pause.)* What am I doing? This is wrong. I've got to stop staring at her. Marcy's going to see and then she'll be upset, and ... and I love her, but ... *(Slight pause.)* But it's so hard not to look.

MARCY. I shouldn't complain. I know I shouldn't. I'm lucky really. Wade is so sweet, but ... I just I wish he'd be more assertive. Every time I ask him a question, it's "Sure. Whatever you want." I can't make all the decisions any more about where we eat or what movie we see. It shouldn't always come down to what I want or ... *(Slight pause.)* I shouldn't complain. Lots of people would love to get everything their way. But I can't take it any more. What's going on in his head? He won't say anything, but he can't always want to see the same movie as me. He can't always feel like having dinner with Tim and Brenda. *(Slight pause.)* I hate the idea that he just goes along with what I want when he might want to do something else. He says everything's fine, but there's part of my brain that keeps screaming at me "He's miserable! He hates French films and thinks Brenda is pretentious. He sacrifices his wants for yours! Can't you see that?" *(Slight pause.)* So, then I'm never happy, because I'm sure he's not. Oh, I can't keep making all the decisions. It's too much responsibility, and I can't take the strain anymore. I want Wade to decide. Can't he stand up and say, "This is what I want, Marcy. I'd like Mexican food tonight." *(Slight pause.)* I think that would be a dream.

WADE. Why am I feeling like this? I mean, I've got a good thing here with Marcy. She adores me. She's sweet. The sex is great. Where is this coming from? I mean, what more could I want? *(Slight pause.)* We don't talk a lot, I guess, but … I don't know what more I'd say. *(Slight pause.)* But is this normal? How can I be suddenly struck like this, and fall for some woman I don't know? I mean, I love Marcy. Don't I? I think I do. But what does "love" feel like anyway? And what is this I'm feeling for this woman I don't even know? Does all this mean my feelings are inconstant? Or am I just a bastard.

NINA. I should tell Frank about this guy. I mean, he keeps staring at me. It's sick. *(Slight pause.)* No, just forget about it. We're getting off soon. No need to make a fuss. And Frank would probably say something or yell at the guy and make a scene. I don't want to ruin the night. It's been so nice.

FRANK. *(Reading the paper.)* Fuckin' politicians.

MARCY. I should tell him. I should say, "Wade, I need you to … " To what? Decide where we eat? That sounds so stupid. Petty. *(Slight pause.)* But is this a sign of something? Does it mean he's just not decisive? Or maybe that he just doesn't feel strongly about anything. That he doesn't know what he really wants or doesn't care, and he's just going whatever direction the wind blows. *(Slight pause.)* And so what does that say about me? I mean, it's been over a year and a half now. Is he thinking marriage or kids, or is he just here because everything is comfortable and easy?

WADE. Okay, I'm not staring at that woman anymore. I won't look that way down the car. I'm acting like some fucking teenager. *(Slight pause.)* But there's just something about her. Maybe it's just the way her hair falls across her face. I don't know. *(Slight pause.)* I'm not looking anymore. *(Slight pause.)* Did she just look at me again? *(Slight pause.)* Maybe she'll get off at our stop.

FRANK. I cannot believe this cocksucker got elected again. I mean, come on. I've got a better command of the English language than this bozo. And how can you vote for a guy who smirks as much as he does? It's like, hello? The man is lying. Can you not see that? *(Slight pause, reacting to Nina.)* What's she doing now? Aw, come on, don't lean against me like that, Nina. Gimme a little room here. I'm trying to read the paper. And stop squeezing my hand all the time. It's really annoying. Like a dripping water faucet when you're trying to fall asleep. Look, here, okay? I'm squeezing your hand back. Now we've both squeezed, and it's all lovey-dovey and you can stop, okay? *(Slight pause, reacting as she squeezes his hand again.)* Aw, crap.

NINA. His hands are so warm. I love that. I love it when he touches me with them. I remember when we first met and shook hands how surprised I was that they were so warm. And rough. I thought I'd hate those rough hands on my stomach or breasts … but I don't.

FRANK. Oh, it's about supporting freedom around the world, huh? Bullshit. Why don't we send troops into Rwanda then? Fuckin' hypocrite, it's about oil, not democracy. Hell, we don't even have a democracy here. Not with these people in charge. We can't have gay marriage or teach evolution, but it's okay to torture prisoners and privatize Social Security. Yeah, 'cause the guys who've created a twelve trillion dollar debt'll really know how to manage the money. Fuck. We might as well hit Vegas and put it all on a spin of the roulette wheel. *(Slight pause, reacting to Nina again.)* Oh, for the love of God, would you not kiss my hand?

MARCY. I worry too much. I think too much. I wish I could just stop my brain. I'd kill for a little silence in my skull, but it never seems to stop. *(Slight pause.)* I should go back into therapy probably. I should go back on medication definitely. I … *(Slight pause.)* Stop. Breathe. Relax. What am I getting so worked up about? There's nothing wrong. Things are good, and I'm worrying about things that aren't important. I talk too much anyway. Wade probably gets overwhelmed by all the things that pour out of my mouth. Who wouldn't be? He's just trying to be considerate by doing the things I want to do. I shouldn't second guess everything. *(Slight pause.)* I should be happy. *(Slight pause.)* I am happy.

WADE. Our stop is next. God, it's killing me to know I'll never see her again. At least if she'd gotten off before us, I'd know which stop is hers. *(Slight pause.)* Unless she lives with her boyfriend. Or they're married. They don't look married. Do they? *(Slight pause.)* Oh, stop! She's just some woman on the train, you idiot. It's a stupid fantasy. Get up and get off the train. You just make yourself unhappy doing this.

MARCY. I am happy. Say it like a mantra. I mean, don't they say that if you smile, it actually makes you feel happy? That something about the muscles being pulled that way, sends a signal back to the brain? How dumb are we? "Huh. I'm smiling. I guess I must be happy." So, say it. Repeat it and pull your lips into a smile … and it'll be real. *(Slight pause.)* It's all right, anyway. Things are good. *(Slight pause.)* I don't care that he was staring at that woman down there. That's just how men are. It doesn't mean anything. Right?

WADE. *(Turning and speaking to Marcy.)* Okay, here we go.

MARCY. *(Looking at Wade and smiling.)* You wanna pick up some ice cream at the store?

WADE. Sure, whatever you want. *(Wade and Marcy exit the train. Nina watches them go and then leans back, relaxing visibly. Nina whispers something to Frank.)*

FRANK. She whispers into my ear, "You can do anything you want with me tonight." And I feel nothing. I mean, that's just sad. When a woman says something like that, and you couldn't give a shit? That's sad. I'm just over this whole thing, I guess. Aw, crap! Her stop is next. She's gonna be pulling me off the train with her and if I try to say no ... Damn it. I'm gonna have to fuck her. And I just want to be alone.

NINA. After that creep got off the train, I could finally relax again. I pull Frank close and bury my face against his neck. I breathe in and smell him. I know pheromones exist for people, because when I get close to him and take a deep breath ... well, it just does something to me. I mean, it's like my brain shuts off. Or the intellectual part does, and I'm left with the animal and ... and there's no words. Or not many. The words I tell him are, "You can do anything you want with me tonight." Which I figure is like verbal pheromones. And he closes his eyes, trying to be cool, but I think I see the corners of his mouth turn up a little. Oh ... I love this man. *(Nina kisses Frank, who smiles and kisses her back. Lights fade to black.)*

End of Play

QUANDARY IN QUANDO

QUANDARY IN QUANDO was produced at Ensemble Studio Theatre in New York City as part of *Whose Country Is It Anyway?* in August 2004. It was directed by Steven Ditmyer. The cast was as follows:

PRESIDENT .... Richard Bey
Karl, an AIDE .... Scott Wood

The play was previously performed at the Workshop at the Neighborhood Playhouse in New York, directed by Steven Ditmyer and performed by Michael Locascio and Michael Simon Hall.

CHARACTERS

PRESIDENT — the President of the United States.
KARL — an aide to the President.

PLACE

The Oval Office in the White House.

TIME

Roughly the present.

QUANDARY IN QUANDO

The Oval Office. The President is leaning back in his chair, feet up on his desk. He is napping, or maybe playing with a child's toy. There is a knock at the door. The President sits up and pretends to be doing some paper work.

PRESIDENT. Yes? *(The door opens and Karl, an aide, enters the room, carrying an official-looking folder.)*

AIDE. Mr. President, there's a developing situation that needs your attention.

PRESIDENT. Damn it. Why does this always happen on a Friday?! I want to go to Camp David this weekend. Is it too much to ask that these things happen on a Monday once in a while? All right, fine. Where's the problem?

AIDE. Quando, sir.

PRESIDENT. Quando, huh? *(Slight pause.)* Where the hell is that? *(The aide extracts a page from the folder he carries and holds it out to the President.)*

AIDE. Well, sir, the island of Quando lies between —

PRESIDENT. Oh, it doesn't matter. What's happening?

AIDE. There's been a revolution.

PRESIDENT. That's terrible! Or were we hoping for one there?

AIDE. No, it's quite a surprise, sir.

PRESIDENT. Who was it? Communists?

AIDE. No —

PRESIDENT. Right Wing extremists?

AIDE. No —

PRESIDENT. An oppressed black majority?

AIDE. No —

PRESIDENT. Some disaffected ethnic group?

AIDE. No, sir, it —

PRESIDENT. Well, spit it out! This isn't twenty questions!

AIDE. Women.

PRESIDENT. What?

AIDE. The entire female population of Quando.

PRESIDENT. Women? Are you sure?

AIDE. The report is quite specific.

PRESIDENT. But ... well, that just can't be. I mean, women don't do things like that. They complain, sure ... but they're not aggressive. Except for those lesbians.

AIDE. These women overran the Quandan Royal Army and defeated the Palace Guards.

PRESIDENT. Unbelievable. Why'd they do it?

AIDE. The report indicates they felt they were being oppressed.

PRESIDENT. Oh, please. Like they don't already have equal rights.

AIDE. Exactly.

PRESIDENT. What?

AIDE. They don't have equal rights.

PRESIDENT. You mean there's the usual bias and sexism.

AIDE. No, sir. The women of Quando can't vote or own property. They're barely acknowledged as citizens.

PRESIDENT. There are still countries like that?

AIDE. Quite a few, sir. Some of our allies even.

PRESIDENT. Really? Who knew? *(Slight pause.)* Still ... that doesn't excuse their actions. I mean, I can't condone violence. There's always a way to talk things out. A lot of people can't vote or own property, but you don't see them revolting.

AIDE. Actually, sir, there have been a few cases of revolutions under those circumstances. And we've even supported some of them. Covertly, of course.

PRESIDENT. Well, yes. Democracy and individual rights are nice, but I'm sure there were other factors at work in those cases. And what's the big deal about the right to vote anyway? Hell, most Americans don't even bother voting. And owning property ... Christ! That's one of the biggest headaches around. Paying property taxes, mortgages, needing special permission to drain all the water out of the "wetland area" that's supposed to be your back yard. These women don't know how good they have it. They can walk the streets without a care.

AIDE. Yes, except one of the things they were protesting was the fact that they can't walk the streets without wearing scarves over their faces.

PRESIDENT. Windy country, is it?

AIDE. No, sir, fundamentalist. Women aren't allowed to show their faces or hair in public.

PRESIDENT. Why not?

AIDE. It's so the men of Quando aren't tempted too much, or caused to have impure thoughts.

PRESIDENT. From looking at their hair?

AIDE. I believe so.

PRESIDENT. What about the rest of their bodies?

AIDE. Completely covered, sir.

PRESIDENT. Good Lord, that's not natural. Thank God women in America have the freedom to walk around wearing next to nothing, and that so many of them take advantage of that freedom. You don't see American men having impure thoughts or losing control.

AIDE. Ah, no, I suppose not. Certain crime statistics not withstanding. But there are women's groups that —

PRESIDENT. Yeah, yeah, yeah. But what's to stop these women from walking down the street without their veil? What're they going to do? Take away their right to vote?

AIDE. Actually, bands of fundamentalists generally grab them off the streets and stone them to death.

PRESIDENT. Oh. *(Slight pause.)* Well, far be it from us to judge other cultures or religions. From their point of view, our ways may seem just as strange to them as theirs do to us.

AIDE. Very broad-minded of you, sir.

PRESIDENT. Well, a President has to pander to … I mean, learn to respect a wide range of opinions. *(Slight pause.)* Okay, give me the numbers. How many dead?

AIDE. None, Mr. President. It was a bloodless revolution.

PRESIDENT. Are you kidding me?! What kind of a revolution doesn't leave dead lying in the streets?! Women! *(Slight pause.)* How about injuries?

AIDE. None mentioned in the report.

PRESIDENT. Ah, ha! So there could be vast numbers of very badly injured, burned and beaten men, hanging onto life by the barest of threads.

AIDE. Ah … well, I suppose that's an outside possibility, sir. But I think if that were the case there'd be something about it in the report. There doesn't seem to have been any violence.

PRESIDENT. So these women … they just walked up to the

Palace and took it over?

AIDE. So it would seem, sir.

PRESIDENT. Well then, they had it coming. What kind of Palace guards don't shoot approaching revolutionaries?!

AIDE. It seems the guards were reluctant to shoot a crowd of unarmed women.

PRESIDENT. Oh, well sure, I can see that. *(Slight pause.)* Hey, you don't suppose ... The Secret Service ... I mean, they'd open fire, right?

AIDE. That would be a judgment call, sir. *(There is a silence.)*

PRESIDENT. This is scary shit, Karl.

AIDE. Yes, sir.

PRESIDENT. We have to do something about this. I mean, we can't allow this sort of chaos to take place.

AIDE. No, sir.

PRESIDENT. We'll have to come to the aid of our long time ally, Quando, and restore the rightful government.

AIDE. Quando is actually not an ally of the U.S.

PRESIDENT. Well, yes, I know that. I mean, Quando our traditional friend, if not formal ally, who —

AIDE. No, they're not even on speaking terms with us. We have no diplomatic ties with Quando. They've never recognized us as a sovereign nation. To them we're still part of the British Empire.

PRESIDENT. What?! Oh, fuck them. Let 'em hang.

AIDE. The Joint Chiefs are very worried about the potentially destabilizing effect this could have. They're worried about a domino effect, sir.

PRESIDENT. *(Pause.)* On the other hand, this is an excellent chance to establish ties with this unique nation. I'm sure we would win the hearts of the people of Quando by restoring their rightfully elected government.

AIDE. Yes, of course. Except the country has been ruled by an age old monarchy. The only one of its kind in the world, in fact. To insure the purity of the blood line, members of the royal family are only allowed to marry other members of the royal family.

PRESIDENT. You mean, like distant cousins and such?

AIDE. Ideally, yes. But over time the genealogy has become a little blurred. It's whatever's available really.

PRESIDENT. And this has been going on for...?

AIDE. Centuries.

PRESIDENT. So the members of this royal family ...

AIDE. Can't even tie their own shoes.

PRESIDENT. Hmm. But I feel sure the people of Quando love the royal family for their simple ways, and have a great affection for them. Just like the English go nuts over the Queen. And I'm sure the good people of Quando want the royal family returned to the palace and have these dictators thrown out on their asses.

AIDE. The revolutionaries aren't dictators. They're extending full citizenship and equal rights to all. They've promised to hold free elections to institute a congress and presidency, modeled after our own.

PRESIDENT. Oh, they are in trouble now. *(Slight pause.)* But these people always promise that sort of thing. "We don't want to stay in power forever. We'll have elections and constitution soon." But then they keep pushing the deadline back.

AIDE. The report says the elections are scheduled for next month and campaigning is under way.

PRESIDENT. Oh. Well, what're our allies saying?

AIDE. What allies, sir?

PRESIDENT. You know, what's-his-face in England.

AIDE. Oh, the Prime Minister said that "The world community looks to America for leadership."

PRESIDENT. You mean they're all too chicken to stick their necks out.

AIDE. Pretty much.

PRESIDENT. Buncha wimps. All right, this is a dire situation which calls for immediate action. If we sit back and allow this sort of thing to happen then where would it end?

AIDE. There's no telling.

PRESIDENT. So we have to nip this in the bud.

AIDE. Yes, sir.

PRESIDENT. The only question remaining is for us to determine the best to impress upon the American people why it is so vitally important that we restore the Quando monarchy.

AIDE. You mean trump up a reason for invading?

PRESIDENT. That would help. I'll tell you one thing, these women were cunning. Pick some country we don't get along with, retard rulers, no one dead. They're kind of limiting our options.

AIDE. Yes, sir.

PRESIDENT. All right, we could say that neighboring countries are worried this revolt will spill over their borders.

AIDE. No, sir. If you'll recall, Quando is an island.

PRESIDENT. Oh-kay. The, ah … the United Nations has asked us to intervene for humanitarian reasons.

AIDE. The U.N. isn't in session.

PRESIDENT. Quando may be developing nuclear weapons and has refused to allow international inspectors into —

AIDE. The only thing they split in Quando is firewood.

PRESIDENT. That never stopped us before. *(Karl just looks at the President.)*

PRESIDENT. All right, all right. How 'bout "Because of the vast untapped oil reserves under — " *(Karl shakes his head.)* Quando is a nation of immense strategic value — *(Karl shakes his head again, and the President stares malevolently at him. There is a silence. Then the President leans forward suddenly.)* Was that the phone?

AIDE. No, sir. It didn't ring.

PRESIDENT. *(Sternly.)* It was the phone. *(He picks up the receiver.)* Hello? Well, hello, Mr. King of Quando. How is everything on your lovely island nation? What? There's been an armed uprising? You've been thrown out of power, just as you were about to establish diplomatic ties with the United States and to bring democracy and prosperity to your people? Why, that's terrible. What can we do to help? Launch a full scale military attack? Hey, you got it. *(He hangs up.)* Karl, I've just had a call from the King of Quando. They have a situation there. Call the Joint Chiefs. Tell them to free Quando.

AIDE. Yes, sir.

PRESIDENT. Great, crisis averted. Anything else?

AIDE. Just a reminder that you have a dinner reception with the League of Women Voters tonight. Or would you like me to cancel that in light of the situation in Quando?

PRESIDENT. What?! Karl, this is an election year! The women voters in this country were the key block that got me elected last time. *(Slight pause.)* You've got a lot to learn about politics. *(Blackout.)*

End of Play

GUNS DON'T KILL

GUNS DON'T KILL was commissioned by the Winter Harbor Theater Company (Caitlin Shetterly, Artistic Director), in Portland, Maine, and performed as part of *Letters to the NRA* in June 2007. It was directed by Caitlin Shetterly, and was performed by Cherie Mason.

The play was subsequently produced by City Theatre, in Miami, Florida as part of their *Summer Shorts* series *UnderShorts* in June 2008. It was directed by James Randolph, and was performed by Sally Biondi.

CHARACTERS

MRS. O'REILLY — a school teacher.

PLACE

A classroom.

TIME

The present.

GUNS DON'T KILL

A primly dressed woman, Mrs. O'Reily, enters and smiles at her classroom of children. She carries some books and a bag or purse.

MRS. O'REILY. Good morning, class. How are you all today? Do you feel all right? I'm so glad to see you, but I'll bet some of you were nervous about coming back to school this morning, yes? Let's see a show of hands.

It's okay to admit you were scared. Even I was a little scared. I mean, not everyone can be brave and resolute like our President was when he sent our soldiers to Iraq. I mean, Iran. No, no, it was … well it was somewhere like that. I'm sure your mommies and daddies talked to you about the terrible shooting at that school. The world can be a scary place, and you can't always predict what might happen. *(Slight pause.)* But none of you have to worry about those things here. Because I bought this. Say hello to my little friend. *(She pulls an automatic pistol out of her bag.)* See? Now if anyone tries to come into our class room and hurt us, we can return fire.

Hmm? Well, now, what's wrong, Juan? Right. Jose. Sorry. But there's nothing to worry about, dear. It's perfectly legal for me to have this small easily concealed pistol whose only purpose is to shoot other human beings. Can anyone tell me why? No? Well, it's thanks to our founding fathers, who in their infinite wisdom added the second amendment to the Constitution, which gives me the right to bear arms.

What's that? No, Duncan it does not mean I have the right to have arms like a bear. Are you being smart with me? Don't forget, I'm armed. *(Slight pause.)* Just kidding. No, "the right to bear arms" means we can all purchase inexpensive handguns like this one, which fits easily into my purse, or pack, or tucked into the back of my pants and hidden under a coat. And thank God for the second amendment, because it means we can protect ourselves from the freaks and sick killers that lurk everywhere. *(Suddenly pointing into a corner.)* Like that one over there!

No, I'm just testing to see who was alert. Duncan, Jose, you failed. You should have hit the ground and covered your head with your hands, not turned and stared into the corner with your mouths hanging open. If there'd been a mad killer there, you'd both be dead. *(Suddenly aiming her gun at the corner.)* Unless I nailed him first! I've been taking lessons. *(Lowering the gun.)* What's that, Jose? Oh. Well, all right, you can go change your pants. But watch out for killers in the hallway. *(She watches Jose leave, then shakes her head a little.)* Where was I? Oh, yes. The second amendment. Can anyone tell me what the Constitution is? Put your hand down, Rachel. I want one of our little foreign students to answer. Since Jose is gone, how about you, Mai? All right, yes, you were born here, but my question still stands. Can you tell me what the Constitution is? No, I didn't think so.

Well, the Constitution is the basis of our wonderful and perfect democracy. And to ensure our rights, the founding fathers added certain items, called amendments, to be very specific about what's right and what's nonsense.

The first amendment is about how we have the freedom of speech and the right to pray to the God you like, even if it's the wrong one. And it says absolutely nothing about the right to burn the American flag, which we all know is wrong, and which has nothing to do with speaking anyway.

Now, who can tell me what the second amendment says? Hmm? Put your hand up, if you do. *(Waving her gun around.)* In fact, everyone put your hands up. No, no, I'm just kidding. Sorry. But, you know, sometimes humor is the best well to deal with grief.

Anyway, the second amendment says, "A well regulated Militia, being necessary to the security of a free State, the right of the people to keep and bear Arms, shall not be infringed." And I think those are the wisest twenty-seven words in the whole Constitution. Now some people will argue about where the commas are placed, or say the use of the word militia means that the framers were talking about an army, or that the word people means "the people of the United States" and not individuals, or point to statistics showing that of all the industrialized, Western nations we have by far the most incidents of gun related violence and murders, and blah, blah, blah.

Well, I say, that's the price of democracy. Why are we free? Because we have guns. All those other amendments, like the freedom of speech, and all those fine words in the Constitution don't mean much without some firepower to back them up. When King George read the Declaration of Independence did he say, "Hey, they're right. Let them be free?" No. It was because we had guns and spent years shooting his soldiers in their bright red coats dead. Did Hitler surrender because we asked him nicely? No. It was because we had guns.

What? All right, Rachel, yes. Technically, Hitler killed himself, but only because our soldiers were about to kick down the door of his bunker. So, you see? No one listens to you unless you have a gun. And then, of course, there's — *(She suddenly wheels about, aiming her gun at someone entering the room.)* Freeze!! Hands on your head, asshole! Down on the ground!

Do it!! You, Duncan, pat him down. Make sure he doesn't have a weapon. No? You're sure?

All right, Juan, you can get up. Yes, yes, Jose, whatever! But you can't just walk in to a room like that. I swear … what? Again? No, you can't go to the bathroom again. I don't care. I think you need to sit down and think about the trouble you've caused.

All right now, everyone settle down. We need to get back to our discussion of … stop it, now. All this crying is just silly. I bet none of you would be crying if you each had an automatic weapon in your little backpacks. So, everyone dry your … I mean it. Class? Settle down. Class! *(She fires a shot into the air and then reacts almost orgasmically.)* God, I love that. Now I know why they say "you'll take this from my cold dead hands." Whew! I may just need to run down to the practice range for a little while so … class dismissed. *(Blackout.)*

End of Play

IN A WORD

IN A WORD was commissioned by the Winter Harbor Theater Company (Caitlin Shetterly, Artistic Director), in Portland, Maine, and performed as part of *Letters to Baghdad* in June 2006. It was directed by Caitlin Shetterly with Craig Pospisil, and was performed by Sarah Jane Casey.

CHARACTERS

CHAR — a woman, 20s, 30s or 40s.

PLACE

A darkened room.

TIME

The present.

IN A WORD

Darkness. Nothing happens for several moments. Then there is a sigh, and a cigarette lighter is lit. It illuminates a woman's face (Char). She stares at the flame for a second, then lights a cigarette, inhaling. She exhales, letting the smoke drift around the flame for a moment, before blowing out the flame. Pause. The tip of the cigarette brightens as Char inhales through it. Pause.

CHAR. I avoid most social functions these days. Or try to. There's just too many damn people there. *(Slight pause.)* And I generally avoid the phone when it rings. It's usually someone I don't want to talk to. With nothing but stupid questions. Like, how am I? *(Slight pause.)* Hell, I avoid the light when I can. There's nothing much I want to see these days. *(Pause.)* But I'm being rude. *(The lights come up slowly and dimly, revealing Char sitting alone in a chair. She holds her cigarette in one hand and an ashtray in the other.)* Sorry. I'm not used to company lately. Conversation's just too draining. Takes too much out of me, trying to talk about … well, about just about anything. Because nothing matters anymore, you know. I mean, look at the world. Nothing means anything, so what's the point in talking? Words are pretty much useless. *(Slight pause.)* I've got no use for them at any rate. I mean, you'd think they were pretty simple things, but no, they come loaded with expectations, obligations, and whatever. Just like people. People who want to stick some neat label on you. But I don't trust them anymore. People or words. They're biased. *(Slight pause.)* What, you think I'm wrong? Just look at the words we use everyday. Male. Female. Man. Woman. Like that's all women are. Extensions of men. Defined by men. The least verbal people on the planet. *(Slight pause.)* And it's not just that. There's waiter, waitress. Actor, actress. It's even our names. Don. Ah. Paul. Ah. George. Ah. I mean, I could go on, but you can think for yourself. Right? *(Slight pause.)* Yeah, I know. You think I'm angry. That I'm a little … "overwrought"? That's what my sister-in-law, Julie says. Well, I've got a word for her too. But since I used it the last time she was here she hasn't come by or called again. *(Slight pause.)* If I knew that was all it'd take, I'd've called her a cunt years ago. *(Slight pause.)* Sorry. Maybe she's right. *(Slight pause.)* But maybe I don't give a fuck. *(Slight pause.)* But really, how many words go the other way? The only one I can think of is widower. Can you think of another word that's female, and you add something to make it male? Widow? That's the word we get? Gee thanks, but you can keep it. *(Slight pause.)* And the definition of that word is a woman without a man. So even the one word we get refers back to men. What is it with you guys? *(Shakes her head, smiling.)* And how many men even call themselves widowers anyway? *(Slight pause.)* Of course, it's usually the men who do the dying first. You make sure of that. So, I guess there's more use for the word widow. *(Slight pause.)* But, like I said, words are pretty useless anymore. They don't tell you anything you don't know the second a man in a uniform appears at your door. *(Slight pause.)* So, I don't need it, okay? I don't want your damn label or anything that comes with it. Okay?! So, just…! *(Pause.)* Just don't call me that. I don't need you to remind me. Like I could forget. *(The lights fade to black, leaving only Char's cigarette. It brightens as she inhales through it. Then it disappears as she stubs it out.)*

End of Play

PERCHANCE

PERCHANCE was produced by the 24 Hour Plays (Tina Fallon, Kurt Gardner, Lindsay Bowen and Philip Naude, producers), at the Atlantic Theater, in New York City, opening on May 7, 2005. It was directed by Mark Lonergan. The cast was as follows:

ROBBIE .... Scott Wood
CASS .... Liz Elkins
ANTONIO .... Matt Saldivar
CYNTHIA, TICKET AGENT
GATE AGENT .... Carla Rzeszewski

CHARACTERS

ROBBIE — a man in his 30s.

CASS — Robbie's girlfriend.

ANTONIO — Cass' lover.

CYNTHIA — Robbie's older sister.

TICKET AGENT and GATE AGENT — airline workers, to be played by the actress playing Cynthia.

PLACE

Various locations: an open space, Robbie's apartment, Cynthia's apartment, an airport.

TIME

The present, more or less.

PERCHANCE

The actors enter and take positions around the stage. Cass, Antonio and Cynthia face away from the audience. Robbie, however, faces the audience.

ROBBIE. It's kind of hazy, but what I remember is: Cass and I are in love. It's not perfect. I'm not going to lie and tell you that. But it was good, and I was happy. I didn't always know I was happy. In fact, sometimes I was downright miserable. And I don't just mean a little blue. I mean really depressed. And I'm not much fun to be around when I'm like that. I get pretty negative, call myself a failure. Things like that. I'm not suicidal or anything. Just depressed. A lot. Like everybody else, really. Just your average New Yorker, who was on Paxil for a while, but didn't like the sexual side effects, so tried Celexa, but that was worse, so then went on Wellbutrin for a couple years, and that was fine, but now is off the medication. *(Slight pause.)* Anyway Cass and I are in love. We live together. We've got a great life, good friends, terrific sex. Cass and me. With each other, not with the friends. As far as I know. *(Slight pause.)* Anyway, one morning — *(Cass turns and faces inward, entering the scene.)*
CASS. I think I'm in love with someone else and I'm moving to San Diego.
ROBBIE. What?!
CASS. Robbie, it just isn't working between the two of us.
ROBBIE. How can you say that?
CASS. Because I think I'm in love with someone else, and I'm moving to San Diego.
ROBBIE. You can't be serious. When did this happen?
CASS. Well, I bought the plane ticket online last night.
ROBBIE. Last night?! You mean, before we went to Chez Josephine for our anniversary?
CASS. No, after that.

ROBBIE. We fell into bed and had sex right after dinner.

CASS. Yeah, it was after that too. I waited until you fell asleep, then I went online and got a really cheap ticket on Last Minute Travel Dot Com. Then I called Antonio.

ROBBIE. Antonio?

CASS. He's this amazing guy I met at that publishing conference in Denver last month. *(Antonio turns and faces the scene. He is suave and self assured.)*

ANTONIO. Hello.

ROBBIE. Then she tells me about Denver. *(Robbie steps back and watches the scene.)*

ANTONIO. You have the look of someone whose life has stagnated and who now longs for a fresh stream in which to swim.

CASS. Oh my god! How did you know?

ANTONIO. It is my gift. So, why does someone so beautiful look so sad?

CASS. I don't know if I can talk about this.

ANTONIO. Very well. I don't mean to intrude.

CASS. *(In a rush.)* You see, the thing is I've been living with my boyfriend, who I love, for four years, and things are great … but they're exactly the same as they were at the beginning.

ANTONIO. And you long for change.

CASS. I don't know. Maybe. I mean, things are good. Sort of. Robbie can be a bit depressed sometimes and that gets old, believe me, but things are okay. It's just that things should change, right?

ANTONIO. Change is the essence of life. To deny change is to deny life itself.

CASS. Exactly. I mean, it's not like I'm one of those women who needs to be married, but after this much time shouldn't we be moving that way? *(Robbie steps forward, addressing Cass.)*

ROBBIE. Wait! I've been thinking about asking you to marry me.

CASS. *(To Robbie.)* Well, how do I know that?

ANTONIO. I would marry you today.

CASS. What?

ROBBIE. You have *got* to be kidding me.

ANTONIO. You have to be bold when you feel a connection like this with another person. I have missed enough chances in my life to know I would rather take a chance than not.

CASS. *(To Robbie.)* I'm going to San Diego. *(Cass and Antonio turn upstage. Robbie turns to the audience again.)*

ROBBIE. And she goes into the bedroom and starts packing. And I … I don't know what to do. My life's just exploded in my face and … and I leave. I walk out the door and just start walking. Until I find myself at my sister's home. *(Cynthia, wearing a robe or dressing gown turns and faces Robbie.)*

CYNTHIA. The kids were a nightmare this morning. Brandie insisted she's going to school in her Cinderella costume from last Halloween, and Andrew couldn't find his English homework. And Joel didn't lift a finger to help me get the kids ready. I mean, I've got work to do too. Maybe it's not a nine to five job like Mr. Advertising, but I've got to turn on the computer and start tapping away. You want some coffee?

ROBBIE. Cass is leaving me.

CYNTHIA. Oh my god. What did you do?

ROBBIE. Me?!

CYNTHIA. Have you been ignoring her?

ROBBIE. No!

CYNTHIA. Have you been all, "Oh, I'm so depressed, and I'm such a failure. Why is everything in my life so terrible"?

ROBBIE. *(Unconvincingly.)* No.

CYNTHIA. Oh, Robbie. What are you going to do?

ROBBIE. What can I do? She's leaving me for this impulsive jerk, who asked her to marry him the same night he met her. *(Slight pause.)* What kills me is I went shopping for an engagement ring while she was in Denver. I was going to propose to her last night.

CYNTHIA. Why didn't you?

ROBBIE. I didn't find a ring I liked.

CYNTHIA. Oh, my god! If you wanted to propose, you should've just proposed! All right, look, if you want her, you've got to do some serious groveling. Where is she?

ROBBIE. On her way to Kennedy.

CYNTHIA. Then you better haul ass. And bring a gift. Something romantic. *(Cynthia turns away. She ditches her robe and quickly ties a colorful scarf around her neck, morphing into a Ticket Agent, as Robbie faces the audience again.)*

ROBBIE. So I run out to go the airport. I think about taking the A train, 'cause it's rush hour and I'm worried about traffic, but I spot a cab and flag it down. *(Slight pause.)* The ride takes forever and costs me sixty bucks but I finally get there. Her flight for San Diego leaves in fifteen minutes, but, of course, I can't get to the gate without a ticket.

TICKET AGENT. Can I help you?

ROBBIE. I'd like a ticket please.

TICKET AGENT. *(Pause, waiting.)* ... for what destination?

ROBBIE. Anywhere.

TICKET AGENT. I'm sorry. I don't understand, sir.

ROBBIE. What's your cheapest ticket to anywhere?

TICKET AGENT. I need a destination, sir.

ROBBIE. Okay, how about Newark?

TICKET AGENT. Newark?

ROBBIE. Fine, ah, Washington. Is there a shuttle to Washington?

TICKET AGENT. Yes.

ROBBIE. Great. One ticket. One way.

TICKET AGENT. One way?

ROBBIE. Yeah, see I just need to get to one of the gates. I'm not really flying anywhere. *(The Ticket Agent stares at him like he's insane or a terrorist or both.)* Kidding. I'm kidding. I'm not a terrorist. Really. Make that round trip. And first class. *(The ticket agent turns away.)* Somehow I get through security in time. *(Cass turns around. She carries a small overnight bag.)*

CASS. Robbie, what are you doing here?

ROBBIE. You can't go.

CASS. Don't do this.

ROBBIE. Please. I love you. *(Antonio turns around and moves to Cass.)*

ANTONIO. My darling. I couldn't wait for your plane to arrive in San Diego, so I flew here overnight so we could begin our new adventure together right away.

ROBBIE. This cannot be happening.

ANTONIO. Who is this?

CASS. This is Robbie.

ANTONIO. *(Suppressing a laugh.)* Yes, I understand your desire for change. *(Turning back to Cass and holding a small glass bottle.)* I brought you a gift. This bottle is full of sand I found on the beaches of Ipanema. Some day I will take you there.

ROBBIE. Hey, I got you a gift too. *(He takes a deck of playing cards out of his pocket. Cass takes them and looks at them, clearly unimpressed.)* It was all they had at the gift shop. *(The Ticket Agent now turns back around as the Gate Agent.)*

GATE AGENT. Ladies and gentlemen, flight 819 for San Diego is ready for boarding. We will begin seating passengers in rows twenty and above.

ANTONIO. Shall we go?

CASS. I'm sorry, Robbie. I love you, but … I have to go.

ROBBIE. Marry me.

CASS. What?

ROBBIE. Marry me. I don't have a ring for you or a bottle of sand, but I love you and I want to spend my life with you. I just want to make you happy. *(Antonio begins pulling Cass away, toward the Gate Agent and the door to the plane.)*

CASS. Robbie, I …

GATE AGENT. Now, boarding all rows. Final boarding call.

ROBBIE. He doesn't love you. He doesn't know you. He doesn't know you like to sleep with that orange teddy bear or that you're always exactly ten minutes late to everything.

ANTONIO. *(To Cass.)* I know the real you. *(Antonio leads Cass away, but she looks back. Robbie follows, handing his ticket to the Gate Agent.)*

GATE AGENT. Ticket please. This ticket is for Washington, D.C., sir.

ROBBIE. I just need to talk to her.

GATE AGENT. I'm sorry, sir. You can't get on this plane. Now, will you go, or do I have to call security?

ROBBIE. Cass! Please don't. *(Robbie tries to get on the plane, but the Gate Agent wrestles him away from the door. Cass tries to move towards Robbie, but Antonio still pulls her away.)*

CASS. Robbie!

ROBBIE. Cass! Marry me!

CASS. Yes! Yes, I'll marry you! *(Robbie and Cass reach for each other. The scene shifts into slow motion as Robbie and Cass break free from the Gate Agent and Antonio, who are slowly spun away, before finally facing upstage in their original positions. Robbie and Cass run towards each other. They do not touch, but spin around each other, somehow missing with Cass turning away, upstage to her original position, and Robbie coming back downstage to face the audience again.)*

ROBBIE. And then I woke up. *(Slight pause.)* It took me a minute, because I'd been in a deep sleep, and you know how it can take a while to get your bearings. What's real, what was the dream. *(Slight pause.)* But then I remember. I never went to the airport or tried to stop her. I never proposed. And she never came back. *(The lights fade on Robbie.)*

End of Play

A QUIET, EMPTY LIFE

A QUIET, EMPTY LIFE was commissioned by the Winter Harbor Theater Company (Caitlin Shetterly, Artistic Director), in Portland, Maine, and performed as part of its production *Letters to the NRA* in June 2007. It was directed by Craig Pospisil and Caitlin Shetterly. The cast was as follows:

NARRATOR .... Jonathan McClain
STEPHANIE .... Joanna Parson

CHARACTERS

NARRATOR — a man in his 30s or 40s.
STEPHANIE — a woman, 30s or 40s, getting dressed.

PLACE

A suburban bedroom.

TIME

The present.

A QUIET, EMPTY LIFE

A woman, Stephanie, enters, half dressed. She approaches a dresser and pulls out articles of clothing, looking them over, comparing them to one another, trying to make a decision. Her mood is somber, and she appears almost to be sleepwalking. She will find clothes to try on, reject, try more and ultimately get dressed by the end. Lights come up on a man standing to one side. He observes Stephanie for a moment, then turns and looks out at the audience.

NARRATOR. Stephanie was not a very political person. Her days did not revolve around the big questions that preoccupied the minds of political leaders and thinkers like, "How can we bring about peace between all people?" or "How can we live in a manner that affords us the luxuries of modern times, but which does not result in harm to the natural world?"

Stephanie lived with her husband Carl and their twin eight-year-old boys in a quiet town far from those larger concerns. Her days were mainly spent worrying about smaller matters like "How can I protect my children from internet porn?" and "When did orange juice get so expensive?"

This afternoon Stephanie found herself standing in her bedroom, pondering a very different question, trying to figure out what to wear. Normally, she wouldn't be faced with a decision like this on a Saturday, but today she had a special function to attend, one that she couldn't get out of, though secretly she longed to. Everyone from the neighborhood would be there, watching her, and she wanted to look right.

Stephanie liked to say she lived in a gated community without the gate. Actually, she and Carl had purchased a modest home in a real estate development not far from the highway that cut through this part of the state. You couldn't see the highway, but you could hear the hum of the truck's tires as they made their way north and south, delivering goods. Their house was at the end of a cul-de-sac, and though she didn't know the term, Stephanie felt its grip.

STEPHANIE. I'm at a dead end.

NARRATOR. She told her therapist, referring to her job as a secretary in a law office. Her therapist said nothing, but merely wrote her a new prescription for anti-depressants. And though she took those pills every day — sometimes twice a day — she never really grasped that the lack of depression did not make her happy.

STEPHANIE. Every time I turn around, I'm still facing the same way.

NARRATOR. She would say as she left his office. That was simply how she felt. It wasn't that her life was hard. Carl was tender and attentive, her boys were wonderful, and she loved her garden. But for some reason there seemed to be a hole in the center of her chest. And so she went on with her life as usual. She went to her job, picked up the twins Nick and Scott from school, and had dinner with them and Carl every night, and continued to feel empty.

Although not as empty as she had felt this past week. Not even a full week. It was Monday that her routine had been disrupted, and though she hated the routine, she knew it was the only thing that kept her moving forward most days. Some afternoons when it was slow at the law office, Stephanie went online and googled the names of ex-boyfriends when she was supposed to be working. Ben Harris was now a contractor outside of Denver, and Mark Lyons wrote for an entertainment magazine. Stephanie suspected Mark was gay. They had only gone all the way once, and it had been a short and sad coupling. Sometimes she felt guilty for trying to find out about these old boyfriends, like she was betraying Carl. It was curiosity more than anything else that drove these inquiries, as she and Carl were very happy, and had rarely had any major arguments in ten years of marriage.

Stephanie had not been at work for the past week, however, and the twins had been home from school. Thankfully, her mother had driven in to lend a hand with things. And now as she stood in front of her closet, Stephanie thought as she often did that she had no good clothes to wear.

Stephanie didn't give much thought to her appearance, wearing the same kind of tops and slacks or blue jeans most days.

In the summer she wore shorts that were a size too large, and which she pulled up too high on her waist, giving her a boxy look. It was a holdover from the hand-me-downs she inherited from her older, larger sisters as a child, and the shorts simply felt right. But it wasn't summer. It was April, and it had been a cold, wet month at that. She would've preferred to wear slacks, but a skirt seemed more appropriate. Her instinct was to wear the black one, but Carl never liked that one, and the appliqué design on it seemed out of place. Carl liked the blue skirt she had, and, though it was a little shorter than she would've wanted, she put it on for him. It wasn't that she didn't want to appear fashionable, but her mind just didn't think along those lines, and the styles of dress that other women wore simply never registered with her. Carl always said she looked good, but she knew he was being nice.

Carl was always being nice, and that drove her crazy. She couldn't stand the way he rolled with all the punches, and tried to find the positive in any bad turn of events. And it made her angry at herself that she felt that way. She knew Carl's attitude was better than hers, and that the worry and stress over things were bad for her health, while Carl's way of thinking was much easier on the system. But she still couldn't understand how it never seemed to upset him when the twins went racing through the house, screaming as they chased each other, or when someone cut them off on the highway. These things sent her blood pressure soaring, and inwardly she cursed at the errant drivers and her own offspring, while Carl would always just smile and say, "Looks like someone's in a hurry."

She wondered over and over how he stayed so even keeled, wishing he'd get to the point where he'd be angry with her, and tell her to stop wasting her time and energy wallowing in depression and therapy, and instead learn to breathe and enjoy their lives together and the jubilant energy that Nick and Scott always seemed to possess. But instead he always smiled and put his warm arms around her when she felt low, and said he would always be there for her. And that always made her feel even worse. And for the thousandth time that day, Stephanie thought about her husband's smile, and fought back her tears.

STEPHANIE. Why?

NARRATOR.   She asked, wondering how something like this could happen in a safe place like Blacksburg, Virginia.

STEPHANIE. Why?

NARRATOR. Why? Why did that boy walk into my classroom and shoot seven people dead. Leaving her alone with the twins to attend my funeral on this bright, but cool April afternoon.

STEPHANIE. Carl? *(Stephanie slowly turns and faces the narrator for the first time, seeing him, perhaps even reaching out to him.)*

NARRATOR. And now that I'm gone and the boring, unfulfilling and empty routine of her wonderful, loving and ultimately oh-so-blissfully-happy life has been destroyed, Stephanie has no idea who will tell her to breathe and enjoy life now. *(The narrator slowly turns and walks away from Stephanie, not looking back, as the lights fade to black.)*

End of Play

MANHATTAN
DRUM-TAPS

MANHATTAN DRUM-TAPS was commissioned by the Metropolitan Playhouse (Alex Roe, Artistic Director), in New York City, and performed as part of *The East Village Chronicles* in January 2004. It was directed by Marie Miller. The cast was as follows:

MARY .... Jane Petrov
HISTORIAN .... Margot Avery
JOHN .... David Mitchell
POET .... Scott Wood

CHARACTERS

MARY— an Irish immigrant.
HISTORIAN — man or woman.
JOHN — an African-American dock worker.
POET — man or woman.

PLACE

A tenement apartment on the Lower East Side of New York.

TIME

July 1863, during the Draft Riots in New York.

MANHATTAN
DRUM-TAPS

*Lights rise on the stage to reveal a room of a tenement apart-
ment on the Lower East Side in July 1863. Mary, a tired young
Irish immigrant, cleans the room. The sounds of a large crowd
of people running by are heard outside. There are voices raised
in anger, but it's hard to hear what's being said. Mary reacts
nervously. The Historian [a man or a woman] enters and
stands in a corner of the stage. He is not in the apartment, and
Mary does not respond to his presence. Whenever the Historian
or the Poet, who enters later, speaks, their speeches occur over
the action detailed in the stage directions before and after
their speeches.*

HISTORIAN. Abraham Lincoln, from his address at Cooper
Union during his first run for the presidency on February 27,
1860: *(Reading.)* Fellow citizens: The facts with which I shall deal
this evening are mainly old and familiar; If there shall be any nov-
elty, it will be in the mode of presenting the facts, and the infer-
ences and observations following that presentation. *(Slight pause.)*
In his speech last autumn, Senator Stephen Douglas said: "Our
fathers, when they framed the Government under which we live,
understood this question of slavery just as well, and even better,
than we do now." I fully indorse this, because it simply leaves the
inquiry: What was the understanding those fathers had of the question mentioned? *(As noted above, Mary's actions takes place during
the preceding speech: Mary moves cautiously toward the entrance to the
front room which faces the street. There is a noise from the back room,
little more than a thump, and Mary turns with a start. She waits.
Nothing happens. After a moment, Mary tentatively goes offstage into
the other room to check on things. She shrieks from offstage and runs*

back on, chased by John, a working class African American man.)
MARY. No! Help! *(John grabs Mary, wrapping one arm around her body and clamping a hand over her mouth. Mary struggles to escape, but John is bigger and stronger. He pulls her down onto the floor and holds her there, still with a hand over her mouth.)*
JOHN. *(In a loud whisper.)* No, no! Be quiet, please! Don't scream!
MARY. *(Muffled.)* Help!
JOHN. No, please! Don't make any noise. I won't hurt you. I promise. But you have to be quiet! *(He pauses. Her struggles cease. She looks up at him, fearful. He looks back at her, equally fearful. Mary struggles to get free from John, forcing him to hold her tighter, even rolling on top of her to restrain her.)*
JOHN. Don't be frightened. I'm not here to hurt you. But you have to be quiet. You understand? If you're quiet, I'll let you go. Yes? *(Mary nods, and John tentatively removes his hand from her mouth. The Poet [man or woman] enters and stands in another corner of the stage. He also goes unnoticed by Mary and John.)*
POET. Walt Whitman first read his poem "Beat! Beat! Drums!" at Pfaff's, a beer garden at Broadway and Bleecker Street, in September 1863. *(Reciting.)*

> First O songs for a prelude,
> Lightly strike on the stretch'd tympanum pride and joy in my city,
> How she led the rest to arms, how she gave the cue,
> How at once with lithe limbs unwaiting a moment she sprang,
> O superb! O Manhattan, my own, my peerless!
> O strongest you in the hour of danger, in crisis! O truer than steel!
> How you sprang — how you threw off the costumes of peace with indifferent hand,
> How you led to the war, that shall serve for our prelude,
> How Manhattan drum-taps led.

(As before, the following action takes place during the preceding speech: Mary doesn't try to speak, so he loosens his grip on her, but he stays ready to restrain and silence her again. They freeze for a moment watching each other. John rolls off her, but he studies her carefully, still ready to pounce. Mary makes no sudden moves to flee or shout. John starts to stand, and Mary begins to scurry away from him across the floor. But she moves too quickly, and John pursues, holding his hands out, ready to grab her, but not yet doing so.)
JOHN. Wait, wait, no! Don't run. Just stay still. *(Mary stops.*

Seeing that she still isn't shouting for help or making a sound, John relaxes a little and straightens up.)

MARY. What do you want?

JOHN. I just need to stay here for a while. I don't mean to scare you. It's just — *(There are more sounds of shouting voices and running feet in the streets outside. John looks toward the sound and then back at Mary.)*

MARY. Get out of here!

JOHN. Shh! Please!

MARY. What do you want?!

JOHN. Not so loud! *(John advances on Mary again, who backs herself against a wall.)*

POET.

> Beat! beat! drums! blow! bugles! blow! Through the windows — through doors — burst like a ruthless force,
>
> Leave not the bridegroom quiet — no happiness must he have now with his bride,
>
> Nor the peaceful farmer any peace, ploughing his field or gathering his grain,
>
> So fierce you whirr and pound you drums — so shrill you bugles blow.

(John comes in close, ready to silence her again, but he does not grab her yet. Mary freezes.)

MARY. Please don't hurt me.

JOHN. I won't, but don't raise your voice. Don't let them know I'm here. Please!

MARY. You stay back.

JOHN. All right, all right. I won't touch you, but just let me stay here 'til they're gone. They'll kill me. Please.

MARY. Why are they chasing you?

JOHN. I don't know. There's no reason. It's … they're rioting. There's thousands I guess, and … it's like a war out there, and … They just want to kill me. *(Slight pause.)* Do you have some water? Could I have some? *(Mary slowly gets to her feet and slides along the wall to a basin with some water. She takes a metal cup from a cupboard and scoops up some water.)*

HISTORIAN. You say you will break up the Union rather than submit to a denial of your Constitutional rights. But no such right is specifically written in the Constitution. That instrument s literally silent about any such right. Neither the word "slave" nor "slavery" is to be found in the Constitution. *(Mary holds the cup out to him, her hand shaking. John crosses to her and takes the cup and drinks.)*

JOHN. Thank you.

MARY. What did you do?

JOHN. Nothing. I didn't do a thing.

MARY. Then why do they want to kill you?

JOHN. Because I'm a Negro.

MARY. You must've done something.

JOHN. No, m'am. I was just walking home.

MARY. Just walking home?

JOHN. Yes.

MARY. Did you say something to someone?

JOHN. No.

MARY. You must have. Did you say something to a white woman?

JOHN. No.

MARY. Did you look at a white woman?

JOHN. I was just walking home.

MARY. Then why did they chase you?

JOHN. Because they can. That's all. Because they can.

MARY. I've heard running and shouting half the day. I went out to the front stoop and saw smoke rising from all different directions. I got scared, didn't know what to think. I've been waiting all day. My husband should've been back hours ago. I don't know where he is, and … I mean, he must be out there somewhere. He … *(Slight pause.)* What's going on out there?

JOHN. It's about the draft, M'am. Because of the war. If you've got three hundred dollars, you can buy your way out of it. But who's got three hundred dollars? So if you don't … you've got to go fight. That's what set them off. Starting fires. All kinds of things.

MARY. Where were you coming from?

JOHN. I work at Fulton Ferry, unloading ships. This morning we couldn't get onto the docks. Longshoremen blocked the way, protesting. Banging pots, carrying signs saying "No Draft!" That's all it was to start. *(Slight pause.)* But it's so hot today. Like you washed yourself in molasses. People got short tempers. I heard a fire company stormed the draft office … and *they* set *it* on fire. And when other fire companies came to put it out, the first ones stopped them. Police tried to break up the crowds, but that just got 'em madder. They started throwing bricks, all kinds of things.

114

(Slight pause.) And then everyone just went into a frenzy. I saw a man, a Negro, pulled off a streetcar and beaten. I don't know if he lived or died. I just turned and started to run. But someone saw me, and shouted "Kill all the niggers!" And they started after me. *(Slight pause.)* Can I have some more water? *(Mary takes his cup and goes to the basin. She about to dip it in the water, but she stops and looks at the cup.)*

HISTORIAN. Holding, as they do, that slavery is morally right, they cannot cease to demand a full national recognition of it, as a legal right. Nor can we justifiably withhold this, on any ground save our conviction that slavery is wrong. If slavery is right, all words, acts, laws, and constitutions against it, are themselves wrong, and should be silenced, and swept away. *(Mary sets the cup down to the side and takes a clean cup to dip in the water basin. She hands John the new cup.)*

JOHN. Thank you. *(Slight pause.)* I had nowhere to go. There's fires everywhere. And the mobs. I couldn't make it home like I wanted. Some of the streets are barricaded by the gangs. Eleventh Street is blocked with carts and whatnot. They put up barriers so the police couldn't get in. But I couldn't get out. *(Slight pause.)* I was a few blocks from here and another mob saw me. Threw rocks. One hit me. And I ran. I just ran whatever way I could. I came around the last corner and ducked between these buildings and got in behind. Your window was open so I slipped inside. I had to. Don't you see? I'm sorry I scared you. I didn't mean to. I swear to God. I wouldn't hurt a soul. I'm just trying to get home to my family. I just want to see my family.

MARY. Your family?

JOHN. Yes.

MARY. My brother is in the fighting. He's somewhere in Pennsylvania. We haven't seen him in six months.

JOHN. I'm sorry to hear that. I hope he's safe.

MARY. He's off fighting your war.

JOHN. It's not my war. It's about secession. The Confederates started it.

MARY. It's about slavery. It's about you people. Lincoln freed you. Why don't you go back to Africa?

JOHN. Back? I've never been there.

MARY. You're not wanted here.

JOHN. Are your people wanted here?

MARY. I'm an American!

JOHN. So am I! I was born in Brooklyn. I'm a free man and always have been. I've never been more than twenty miles from this island. *(John faces off against Mary, who shrinks away from him. John softens a bit.)*

POET.
> How the true thunder bellows after the lightning — How bright the flashes of lightning!
>
> How Democracy with desperate vengeful port strides on, shown through the dark by those flashes of lightning!
>
> I have witness'd the true lightning, I have witness'd my cities electric,
>
> I have lived to behold man burst forth and warlike America rise.

(John holds out the cup to Mary, who takes it gingerly and sets it next to the first cup he drank from.)

MARY. Fine. You got away. You hid here. Now go. Get out.

JOHN. I can't yet.

MARY. I don't want you in my house.

JOHN. I can't. They're still out there.

MARY. I don't hear anyone.

JOHN. Maybe they're not right outside your door, but they're all over the streets. If they see me, they'll kill me.

MARY. Maybe not.

JOHN. They had clubs. And rope.

MARY. Then maybe they've gone on to something else. Forgotten about you.

JOHN. Mobs are short on reason, but long on memory.

MARY. I don't want you here! Get out! If someone sees you in here with me …

JOHN. Shh, shh … so we'll be quiet. Yes? We'll be very quiet. And I won't touch you. I won't hurt you. All right?

MARY. No, you have to go.

JOHN. Are you listening to me?

MARY. Yes, but my husband is out there. He works on the docks too. He could be one of the people chasing you. I don't want him walking in and finding you here with me.

JOHN. Can't you just let me stay a little while?

MARY. I have been. You've been hiding here. Keeping me a prisoner in my own home. But someone could've seen you come in. They could tell people. My husband could be home any time. It's

116

not safe for you to be here.

JOHN. But —

MARY. I'll scream.

JOHN. Don't.

MARY. Then leave.

JOHN. I can't. *(Mary shrieks. John jumps her and they struggle. Mary continues to cry out, and John hits her.)*

POET.

> Beat! beat! drums! — blow! bugles! blow!
> Mind not the timid - mind not the weeper or prayer,
> Let not the child's voice be heard, nor the mother's entreaties,
> So strong you thump O terrible drums — so loud you bugles blow.

(Mary falls and is quiet. John pounces on her, holding her still.)

JOHN. All I did was ask you to be quiet! Said I wouldn't touch you. All you had to do was be quiet!

MARY. All right.

JOHN. Now, I'm sorry, m'am, but what could I do? I want to leave here. But I can't right now! *(Mary nods. John releases her and stands. She sits up, clutches a hand to the side of her face where John struck her.)*

HISTORIAN. If it is right, we cannot justly object to its nationality — if it is wrong, they cannot justly insist upon its enlargement. All they ask, we could readily grant, if we thought slavery right. *(John goes to the water basin, finds a hand towel and soaks it in the water. Mary watches him, very still. He wrings out some of the water and brings the towel back to her and carefully daubs her cheek with the cool towel. She looks at him hard. John stops. Mary reaches up and takes hold of the towel. He releases it, stands and walks away. Mary holds the towel to her face as she slowly gets to her feet.)*

JOHN. I'm sorry. Does it hurt?

MARY. Yes.

JOHN. I'm sorry.

MARY. I'm all right.

JOHN. I just want to get home to my wife and little girl.

MARY. I believe you.

JOHN. Do you?

MARY. Yes.

JOHN. I'm sorry.

MARY. I don't hear anything. Maybe the streets are clear.

JOHN. I don't know.

MARY. I can look out front.

JOHN. *(Long pause.)* All right. *(Mary exits to the front room. John waits, tense, expecting to hear her call out to the mob.)*

HISTORIAN. Thinking it right, they are not to blame for desiring its full recognition, but, thinking it wrong, as we do, can we yield to them? Can we cast our votes with their view, and against our own? *(Mary returns. She dips the towel in the water basin again. Wrings it out. John watches her.)*

MARY. There's a crowd about two blocks to the east. But they're moving away. Towards the river.

JOHN. Are you sure?

MARY. If you slip out the back and go through the yards and out onto Ninth Street you could go west. And get away.

JOHN. Thank you. *(Slight pause.)* I'm sorry.

MARY. Just go. And good luck getting home.

JOHN. Thank you. God bless you.

POET.

O Captain! my Captain! our fearful trip is done,

The ship has weather'd every rack, the prize we sought is won,

The port is near, the bells I hear, the people all exulting.

(John hurries out into the back room. Mary touches her face to feel the welt on her cheek. The sound of the crowd returns, with raised voice heard from the front of the building. Mary turns and walks purposefully to the front room.)

HISTORIAN. Let us be diverted by none of those sophistical contrivances such as groping for some middle ground between the right and the wrong Let us have faith that right makes might, and in that faith, let us to the end, dare to do our duty as we understand it. *(Mary is heard calling out to the mob.)*

MARY. *(Offstage.)* He's in the back! The nigger's out back here! *(The lights fade on the room, but two spots remains on the Poet and Historian.)*

POET.

O Captain! my Captain! our fearful trip is done,

But O heart! heart! heart!

O the bleeding drops of red!

Where on the deck my Captain lies,

Fallen cold and dead.

(The lights on the Poet and Historian fade to black.)

End of Play

PROPERTY LIST

ON THE WINGS OF A BUTTERFLY
  Spiral notebook

FREE
  Briefcase
  Man's tie
  Shirt
  Jacket
  Shoes
  Socks
  Pants
  Underwear
  Woman's coat
  Other women's articles of clothing

WHAT PRICE?
  File Folder
  Recording device
  Pen
  Cell phone

NO CHILD LEFT
  Armload of books

GUERILLA GORILLA
  Money
  Badge
  Handcuffs
  Small canister of pepper spray
  Gun

TRAIN OF THOUGHT
  Newspaper

QUANDRY IN QUANDO
  Paperwork on desk
  Official-looking folder with documents inside
  Telephone

GUNS DON'T KILL
  Automatic pistol

IN A WORD
  Cigarette lighter
  Cigarette
  Ashtray

PERCHANCE
  Colorful scarf
  Overnight bag
  Small bottle filled with sand
  Deck of playing cards

A QUIET EMPTY LIFE
  Some articles of women's clothing

MANHATTAN DRUM-TAPS
  Metal cup
  Water
  Hand towel

SOUND EFFECTS

MANHATTAN DRUM TAPS
A thumping noise from back room
Shouting voices
Running feet

NEW PLAYS

★ **GUARDIANS by Peter Morris.** In this unflinching look at war, a disgraced American soldier discloses the truth about Abu Ghraib prison, and a clever English journalist reveals how he faked a similar story for the London tabloids. "Compelling, sympathetic and powerful." *–NY Times.* "Sends you into a state of moral turbulence." *–Sunday Times (UK).* "Nothing short of remarkable." *–Village Voice.* [1M, 1W] ISBN: 978-0-8222-2177-7

★ **BLUE DOOR by Tanya Barfield.** Three generations of men (all played by one actor), from slavery through Black Power, challenge Lewis, a tenured professor of mathematics, to embark on a journey combining past and present. "A teasing flare for words." *–Village Voice.* "Unfailingly thought-provoking." *–LA Times.* "The play moves with the speed and logic of a dream." *–Seattle Weekly.* [2M] ISBN: 978-0-8222-2209-5

★ **THE INTELLIGENT DESIGN OF JENNY CHOW by Rolin Jones.** This irreverent "techno-comedy" chronicles one brilliant woman's quest to determine her heritage and face her fears with the help of her astounding creation called Jenny Chow. "Boldly imagined." *–NY Times.* "Fantastical and funny." *–Variety.* "Harvests many laughs and finally a few tears." *–LA Times.* [3M, 3W] ISBN: 978-0-8222-2071-8

★ **SOUVENIR by Stephen Temperley.** Florence Foster Jenkins, a wealthy society eccentric, suffers under the delusion that she is a great coloratura soprano—when in fact the opposite is true. "Hilarious and deeply touching. Incredibly moving and breathtaking." *–NY Daily News.* "A sweet love letter of a play." *–NY Times.* "Wildly funny. Completely charming." *–Star-Ledger.* [1M, 1W] ISBN: 978-0-8222-2157-9

★ **ICE GLEN by Joan Ackermann.** In this touching period comedy, a beautiful poetess dwells in idyllic obscurity on a Berkshire estate with a band of unlikely cohorts. "A beautifully written story of nature and change." *–Talkin' Broadway.* "A lovely play which will leave you with a lot to think about." *–CurtainUp.* "Funny, moving and witty." *–Metroland (Boston).* [4M, 3W] ISBN: 978-0-8222-2175-3

★ **THE LAST DAYS OF JUDAS ISCARIOT by Stephen Adly Guirgis.** Set in a time-bending, darkly comic world between heaven and hell, this play reexamines the plight and fate of the New Testament's most infamous sinner. "An unforced eloquence that finds the poetry in lowdown street talk." *–NY Times.* "A real jaw-dropper." *–Variety.* "An extraordinary play." *–Guardian (UK).* [10M, 5W] ISBN: 978-0-8222-2082-4

DRAMATISTS PLAY SERVICE, INC.
440 Park Avenue South, New York, NY 10016   212-683-8960   Fax 212-213-1539
postmaster@dramatists.com   www.dramatists.com

NEW PLAYS

★ **THE GREAT AMERICAN TRAILER PARK MUSICAL music and lyrics by David Nehls, book by Betsy Kelso.** Pippi, a stripper on the run, has just moved into Armadillo Acres, wreaking havoc among the tenants of Florida's most exclusive trailer park. "Adultery, strippers, murderous ex-boyfriends, Costco and the Ice Capades. Undeniable fun." *–NY Post.* "Joyful and unashamedly vulgar." *–The New Yorker.* "Sparkles with treasure." *–New York Sun.* [2M, 5W] ISBN: 978-0-8222-2137-1

★ **MATCH by Stephen Belber.** When a young Seattle couple meet a prominent New York choreographer, they are led on a fraught journey that will change their lives forever. "Uproariously funny, deeply moving, enthralling theatre." *–NY Daily News.* "Prolific laughs and ear-to-ear smiles." *–NY Magazine.* [2M, 1W] ISBN: 978-0-8222-2020-6

★ **MR. MARMALADE by Noah Haidle.** Four-year-old Lucy's imaginary friend, Mr. Marmalade, doesn't have much time for her—not to mention he has a cocaine addiction and a penchant for pornography. "Alternately hilarious and heartbreaking." *–The New Yorker.* "A mature and accomplished play." *–LA Times.* "Scathingly observant comedy." *–Miami Herald.* [4M, 2W] ISBN: 978-0-8222-2142-5

★ **MOONLIGHT AND MAGNOLIAS by Ron Hutchinson.** Three men cloister themselves as they work tirelessly to reshape a screenplay that's just not working—*Gone with the Wind.* "Consumers of vintage Hollywood insider stories will eat up Hutchinson's diverting conjecture." *–Variety.* "A lot of fun." *–NY Post.* "A Hollywood dream-factory farce." *–Chicago Sun-Times.* [3M, 1W] ISBN: 978-0-8222-2084-8

★ **THE LEARNED LADIES OF PARK AVENUE by David Grimm, translated and freely adapted from Molière's *Les Femmes Savantes.*** Dicky wants to marry Betty, but her mother's plan is for Betty to wed a most pompous man. "A brave, brainy and barmy revision." *–Hartford Courant.* "A rare but welcome bird in contemporary theatre." *–New Haven Register.* "Roll over Cole Porter." *–Boston Globe.* [5M, 5W] ISBN: 978-0-8222-2135-7

★ **REGRETS ONLY by Paul Rudnick.** A sparkling comedy of Manhattan manners that explores the latest topics in marriage, friendships and squandered riches. "One of the funniest quip-meisters on the planet." *–NY Times.* "Precious moments of hilarity. Devastatingly accurate political and social satire." *–BackStage.* "Great fun." *–CurtainUp.* [3M, 3W] ISBN: 978-0-8222-2223-1

DRAMATISTS PLAY SERVICE, INC.
440 Park Avenue South, New York, NY 10016 212-683-8960 Fax 212-213-1539
postmaster@dramatists.com www.dramatists.com

NEW PLAYS

★ **AFTER ASHLEY by Gina Gionfriddo.** A teenager is unwillingly thrust into the national spotlight when a family tragedy becomes talk-show fodder. "A work that virtually any audience would find accessible." *–NY Times.* "Deft characterization and caustic humor." *–NY Sun.* "A smart satirical drama." *–Variety.* [4M, 2W] ISBN: 978-0-8222-2099-2

★ **THE RUBY SUNRISE by Rinne Groff.** Twenty-five years after Ruby struggles to realize her dream of inventing the first television, her daughter faces similar battles of faith as she works to get Ruby's story told on network TV. "Measured and intelligent, optimistic yet clear-eyed." *–NY Magazine.* "Maintains an exciting sense of ingenuity." *–Village Voice.* "Sinuous theatrical flair." *–Broadway.com.* [3M, 4W] ISBN: 978-0-8222-2140-1

★ **MY NAME IS RACHEL CORRIE taken from the writings of Rachel Corrie, edited by Alan Rickman and Katharine Viner.** This solo piece tells the story of Rachel Corrie who was killed in Gaza by an Israeli bulldozer set to demolish a Palestinian home. "Heartbreaking urgency. An invigoratingly detailed portrait of a passionate idealist." *–NY Times.* "Deeply authentically human." *–USA Today.* "A stunning dramatization." *–CurtainUp.* [1W] ISBN: 978-0-8222-2222-4

★ **ALMOST, MAINE by John Cariani.** This charming midwinter night's dream of a play turns romantic clichés on their ear as it chronicles the painfully hilarious amorous adventures (and misadventures) of residents of a remote northern town that doesn't quite exist. "A whimsical approach to the joys and perils of romance." *–NY Times.* "Sweet, poignant and witty." *–NY Daily News.* "Aims for the heart by way of the funny bone." *–Star-Ledger.* [2M, 2W] ISBN: 978-0-8222-2156-2

★ **Mitch Albom's TUESDAYS WITH MORRIE by Jeffrey Hatcher and Mitch Albom, based on the book by Mitch Albom.** The true story of Brandeis University professor Morrie Schwartz and his relationship with his student Mitch Albom. "A touching, life-affirming, deeply emotional drama." *–NY Daily News.* "You'll laugh. You'll cry." *–Variety.* "Moving and powerful." *–NY Post.* [2M] ISBN: 978-0-8222-2188-3

★ **DOG SEES GOD: CONFESSIONS OF A TEENAGE BLOCKHEAD by Bert V. Royal.** An abused pianist and a pyromaniac ex-girlfriend contribute to the teen-angst of America's most hapless kid. "A welcome antidote to the notion that the *Peanuts* gang provides merely American cuteness." *–NY Times.* "Hysterically funny." *–NY Post.* "The *Peanuts* kids have finally come out of their shells." *–Time Out.* [4M, 4W] ISBN: 978-0-8222-2152-4

DRAMATISTS PLAY SERVICE, INC.
440 Park Avenue South, New York, NY 10016 212-683-8960 Fax 212-213-1539
postmaster@dramatists.com www.dramatists.com

NEW PLAYS

★ **RABBIT HOLE by David Lindsay-Abaire.** Winner of the 2007 Pulitzer Prize. Becca and Howie Corbett have everything a couple could want until a life-shattering accident turns their world upside down. "An intensely emotional examination of grief, laced with wit." *—Variety.* "A transcendent and deeply affecting new play." *—Entertainment Weekly.* "Painstakingly beautiful." *—BackStage.* [2M, 3W] ISBN: 978-0-8222-2154-8

★ **DOUBT, A Parable by John Patrick Shanley.** Winner of the 2005 Pulitzer Prize and Tony Award. Sister Aloysius, a Bronx school principal, takes matters into her own hands when she suspects the young Father Flynn of improper relations with one of the male students. "All the elements come invigoratingly together like clockwork." *—Variety.* "Passionate, exquisite, important, engrossing." *—NY Newsday.* [1M, 3W] ISBN: 978-0-8222-2219-4

★ **THE PILLOWMAN by Martin McDonagh.** In an unnamed totalitarian state, an author of horrific children's stories discovers that someone has been making his stories come true. "A blindingly bright black comedy." *—NY Times.* "McDonagh's least forgiving, bravest play." *—Variety.* "Thoroughly startling and genuinely intimidating." *—Chicago Tribune.* [4M, 5 bit parts (2M, 1W, 1 boy, 1 girl)] ISBN: 978-0-8222-2100-5

★ **GREY GARDENS book by Doug Wright, music by Scott Frankel, lyrics by Michael Korie.** The hilarious and heartbreaking story of Big Edie and Little Edie Bouvier Beale, the eccentric aunt and cousin of Jacqueline Kennedy Onassis, once bright names on the social register who became East Hampton's most notorious recluses. "An experience no passionate theatergoer should miss." *—NY Times.* "A unique and unmissable musical." *—Rolling Stone.* [4M, 3W, 2 girls] ISBN: 978-0-8222-2181-4

★ **THE LITTLE DOG LAUGHED by Douglas Carter Beane.** Mitchell Green could make it big as the hot new leading man in Hollywood if Diane, his agent, could just keep him in the closet. "Devastatingly funny." *—NY Times.* "An out-and-out delight." *—NY Daily News.* "Full of wit and wisdom." *—NY Post.* [2M, 2W] ISBN: 978-0-8222-2226-2

★ **SHINING CITY by Conor McPherson.** A guilt-ridden man reaches out to a therapist after seeing the ghost of his recently deceased wife. "Haunting, inspired and glorious." *—NY Times.* "Simply breathtaking and astonishing." *—Time Out.* "A thoughtful, artful, absorbing new drama." *—Star-Ledger.* [3M, 1W] ISBN: 978-0-8222-2187-6

DRAMATISTS PLAY SERVICE, INC.
440 Park Avenue South, New York, NY 10016 212-683-8960 Fax 212-213-1539
postmaster@dramatists.com www.dramatists.com